Understanding
the Land of the Bible

Understanding
the Land of the Bible
A Biblical-Theological Guide

O. Palmer Robertson

P U B L I S H I N G
P. O. BOX 817 • PHILLIPSBURG • NEW JERSEY 08865

Unless otherwise indicated, Scripture quotations are from the HOLY BIBLE, NEW INTERNATIONAL VERSION. Copyright © 1973, 1978, 1984 International Bible Society. Used by permission of Zondervan Bible Publishers. Italics indicate emphasis added.

Printed in the United States of America

Library of Congress Cataloging-in-Publication Data

Robertson, O. Palmer
    Understanding the land of the Bible: a biblical-theological guide
/O. Palmer Robertson.
      p.   cm.
    Includes bibliographical references and indexes.
    ISBN 0-87552-399-4 (pbk.)
    1. Bible—Geography. 2. Palestine—Historical geography.
I. Title
BS630.R57 1996
220.9'1—dc20   96-33675

Contents

Preface

Many experiences and many people go into the writing of a book. It hardly would be possible to reconstruct all the details that have contributed to the shaping of the current work. Yet some people deserve credit, and some circumstances may enlighten the reading of this material.

Readers may be surprised to find a "missionary" thrust in a book about the land of the Bible. One obvious reason for this outlook is the fact that Scripture repeatedly emphasizes that this land was chosen by God just because of its ability to serve as a springboard to all the nations of the world. But another explanation must be included as well. For at the time of the writing of this book, the author and his wife were involved personally in missionary teaching among the wonderful people of the little country of Malawi, appropriately known as "the warm heart of Africa." From that perspective, it was impossible to ignore the witness of Scripture concerning the significance of the land of the Bible in God's purpose to reach all nations of the world with the saving gospel of his Son.

The orderings of God's providence also were evident in the people that have contributed directly or indirectly to this work. First, there was Gordon Franz of the American Institute of Holy Land Studies in Jerusalem, who led us from Dan to Beersheba and beyond. Apart from his expert guidance and commentary, we never would have seen all the wonders of the "beautiful land."

Second, there was John D. Currid of the faculty of Reformed Theological Seminary in Jackson, Mississippi. Dr. Currid has been gracious enough to employ his expertise in writing the chapter on climate and vegetation, and in supplying the numerous footnotes dealing with archaeological matters.

Finally there was (and always will be) my wife, Julia. She climbed the highest mountains, endured the desert heat, and made a happy time out of sometimes Spartan circumstances. She even drove long hours as I composed the bulk of the manuscript on our battery-powered computer. Without her constant companionship, this work would not have been done.

Special thanks are due the management, staff, and editors of Presbyterian and Reformed Publishing Company for their willingness to employ their numerous skills in seeing this project to the end. I am sure they join with me in hoping that this work will build the confidence of God's people in the Lord's commitment to bring to final completion the great work of redemption that he has begun.

O. Palmer Robertson

Introduction

From the earliest days of the Christian church until today, guides have been written to introduce readers and travelers to the land of the Bible. As early as the third century, Eusebius, bishop of Caesarea, wrote his *Onomasticon,* which describes the land of the Bible through the eyes of a person living in Palestine very early in the history of Christianity. Mark Twain in his *The Innocents Abroad* paints an extensive but highly unappreciative picture of Canaan's "supposed" beauties from the perspective of a traveled American author. A more technical treatment of the land was popularized with George Adam Smith's *The Historical Geography of the Holy Land,* first published in 1894. The latter half of the twentieth century has seen a more scientific approach to the analysis of the land in works such as Yohanan Aharoni's *The Land of the Bible: A Historical Geography* (1962).

But in all these works, very few attempts have been made to explain the distinctive truths concerning God's redemptive purposes that the various features of the land itself serve to reinforce. All these land guides focus principally on the historical and geographical features of the land, rather than observing the significance that various portions of the land have played in the history of redemption.[1] But a reader cannot go far into the documents of either the old covenant or the new without noting the function of various aspects of creation in reinforcing truths about redemption. Adam begins life in a garden, John the Baptist summons men into the wilderness, and Jerusalem is situated on a mountain. Scripture itself makes the natural connection between the blessings of a garden and the testings of a wilderness, the exaltations of a mountain's high elevation and the humiliations of a valley's

---

1. A noteworthy exception to this general absence of reflection on the theological significance of the land is Walter Brueggemann's *The Land* (Philadelphia: Fortress Press, 1977). Brueggemann's work actually is a *tour de force* that attempts to reorient the whole of biblical history and theology with "land" as the central factor. In the opening chapter he states: "Israel's faith is essentially a journeying in and out of the land, and its faith can be organized around these focuses" (p. 14). One chapter explains the whole of Israel's law, including the Ten Commandments, in terms of its significance for the land. Even the crucifixion of Christ is interpreted in terms of land-loss (p. 180).

Brueggemann's work includes many stimulating proposals. Israel's national life is judged in terms of the vitality of its faith in God's gift of the land. The barrenness of Israel's experience in the wilderness is related theologically to the barrenness of the wives of the patriarchs (p. 29). The call of the exiles to return to the land is interpreted as a resurrection motif (p. 180). These seminal ideas deserve careful consideration.

At the same time, Brueggemann appears to be overly influenced by modern philosophies about the social significance of land and its possession. Though qualifying his perspective by reference to the importance of Torah in Israel's land-management, he states that the possession of land "required" a new kind of communication from David as king (p. 81). This new form of communication only "dispatched and commanded," rather than actually communicating with the people. In reflecting on Israel's prospect of exile, he states, "Have we that to learn from Marx, that being in land without caring for community ends history?" (p. 111). It would seem obvious that this statement was made before the full exposé of European communism through its collapse at the end of the twentieth century. In that light it hardly could be said that Marxism taught a theory of land-management that "cared" for the people.

deep depressions. These "values" connected to the natural orderings of creation never appear fantastic or forced. Instead, they confirm the unity and order arising from the one God's single purpose in all his workings in the world.

The present guide offers an introductory overview of the geographical features of the land of the Bible, noting how those diverse elements affected biblical history. In addition, it points out the role certain features of the land have played in God's purposes in redemptive history. This perspective may provide the answers to certain questions that could not be discovered any other way, such as:

- What is significant about this land's position at the eastern end of the Mediterranean Sea?
- Why was it so important that a "wilderness" terrain should wrap around the southeastern portion of the land of the Bible?
- What factors of geography as well as ancient Israelite history led Joshua to direct his people toward Shechem as soon as the central portion of the land had been claimed?
- What is the relation of Jesus' beginning his ministry in Capernaum to the worldwide dimensions of the Christian Gospel?

These questions, along with others, may find their fullest answer in the significance of the land of the Bible for the plans and purposes of God. By considering this perspective, the reader may come to appreciate more fully the Lord's designation of this particular locale as the place for the outworking of his redemptive purposes.

It was not by accident that this particular land with its distinctive locale and its unique features became the stage for the unfolding drama of redemption. The Lord himself declares that he deliberately set Jerusalem "in the center of the nations, with countries all around her" (Ezek. 5:5). According to the song of Moses, when the Most High gave the nations their inheritance, he set up the boundaries of the various peoples "according to the number of the sons of Israel" (Deut. 32:8). So let us allow this land in its uniqueness to reinforce for us today the truths that bring salvation for men.

PART ONE

AN OVERVIEW
OF THE LAND

Looking simply through the eyes of the curious first-time traveler, the land of the Bible is a wondrous realm of spectacular contrasts. The Lord himself calls it the "land I had searched out for them, a land flowing with milk and honey, the most beautiful of all lands" (Ezek. 20:6). Elsewhere it is called "a good land" (Deut. 8:7), "the Beautiful Land" (Dan. 8:9; 11:16), "a delightful land" (Mal. 3:12), "the pleasant land" (Ps. 106:24; cf. Hos. 9:13), and "a desirable land, the most beautiful inheritance of any nation" (Jer. 3:19). Compacted into a territory no more than fifty miles wide and 150 miles long are mountain peaks snowcapped year-round and a depression so deep that it holds the distinction of being the lowest place on earth. To the west of this land are the shores of the Mediterranean, and to the east the desert of Arabia. Fertile valleys of Galilee contrast with stark mountainous terrain in the Negev. In chapters 1–3 we shall look at the land of the Bible first as a whole and then in its parts, from west to east and from south to north. These various parts of the land may be viewed from the perspective of their distinctive roles in the history of redemption.

CHAPTER ONE

THE LAND AS A WHOLE

"Land" as a factor of theological significance begins with "Paradise." The original Garden embodied the perfection of God's blessing on the newly created man as a place for him to dwell. This original "land" provided abundant sustenance for life and comfortable space for habitation. In this "land" called "Paradise" man could serve his God and find meaningful purpose for life.

As a consequence of the alienation from God caused by their willful rebellion, the first man and woman found themselves ejected from this land of bliss. As fallen man traversed the earth, his alienation from the world about him was reinforced at every point. His environment had become his enemy. Everywhere thorns and thistles flourished.

But a divine promise gave him hope. There was a "land,"

a land flowing with milk and honey. Somewhere ahead of him he would find it, for God had purposed to redeem man from the curse, to restore him to the land of blessing he had lost.

This glimpse of hope found concrete expression in the promise given to Abraham. As a supreme act of faith, the Patriarch abandoned the land of his fathers and became a wandering stranger, always on the move toward a "land" that God had promised. His sojourn was a perfect picture of the journey to paradise that the redeemed must undertake. Man must leave his own familiar environment and travel by faith in God's promises of redemption toward a land in the world as it was to be.

Abraham arrived at the land but never possessed it. He saw with his own eyes the place of promised restoration, but he died owning no more than a family burial plot (Gen. 23:17–20). His whole life-experience forced him to look beyond the present temporal circumstance in which he lived to "the city which has foundations, whose builder and maker is God" (Heb. 11:10 NKJV).

To Moses and the people of his generation, God renewed the promise of restoration to the land. On the other side of the desert, a land flowing with milk and honey was waiting for them. But Moses and his contemporaries wandered in the wilderness of Sinai for forty years, and Moses died in faith, not having received the promise (Heb. 11:39).

Under Joshua's generalship the people conquered the land, receiving in a limited fashion the paradise God had promised. But it quickly became obvious that this territory could not be the ultimate paradise. Undefeated Canaanites remained as "hornets" to remind Israel of its own imperfections, as well as the limitations of the land itself; for how could a full-fledged return to the land of paradise be realized apart from the perfection-in-holiness of its inhabitants? Yet, through the large object lesson that was the land of the Canaanites, each successive generation learned to live in hope, not having possessed the promise in the fullest sense.

The imagery of a fruitfulness equaling paradise did not

come to its fullest realization until the era of Israel's united monarchy. The anointed king reigned over the whole of the land, and his people enjoyed the blessings of prosperity. Eventually, under Solomon, Israel claimed the land from the Euphrates to the border of Egypt, just as the Lord had promised originally to Abraham (Gen. 15:18; Ex. 23:31; cf. 1 Kings 4:21; 8:65; 2 Chron. 9:26). The peace and prosperity enjoyed under Solomon's reign was described as a situation in which every man was sitting "under his own vine and fig tree" (1 Kings 4:25), an idealized picture of harmony among man, his God, and his environment. The prophets extended this same imagery of paradise into the distant future, pointing to the day when every man would enjoy the tranquillity of sitting under his own vine and fig tree (Mic. 4:4; Zech. 3:10).

But the united monarchy was not by any means a perfect situation, and it could not last forever. After Solomon, the Davidic line, anticipating the rule of Israel's "messiah," continued only in the kingdom of Judah. Nevertheless, it endured for four hundred years, which has proved to be one of the longest dynasties in the history of humanity. But because of the persistent sin of God's people, and because the old covenant possessed the nature of predictive anticipation of future blessings, this picture of a restored paradise eventually had to come to an end.

The land was devastated, the people banished. Persistently disregarding God's laws, they came to be known as *lo-ammi*, meaning "not-my-people" (Hos. 1:9). The fruitful land took on the appearance of a desert, a dwelling place of jackals, owls, and scorpions. The people were dragged in chains to the ancient locale of their forefathers, being forced to return to the era before God's call had come to Abraham. Paradise, even in its old covenant shadow form, was taken from them.

Yet, contrary to a common misimpression, the history of the old covenant does not end with exile. God's people are not left outside the land. Instead, they return to the Land of Promise before the curtain falls to end the old covenant era.

Their return is for them a kind of resurrection from the dead, a renewal of the life they had lost. Ezekiel's vision of the valley of dry bones that come to life anticipates a restoration to the Land of Promise, but also envisions resurrection from the dead. God shall breathe the breath of life into those bleached, brittle bones (Ezek. 37:4–6). The scattered people shall come back to life. They shall return to the land, for the Lord declares,

O my people, I am going to open your graves and bring you up from them; I will bring you back to the land of Israel. Then you, my people, will know that I am the Lord, when I open your graves and bring you up from them. I will put my Spirit in you and you will live, and I will settle you in your own land. (Ezek. 37:12–14)

The small portion of the "land" that Israel returned to possess after the Babylonian captivity was minuscule when compared to the expansive territory claimed by Solomon five hundred years earlier. Fewer than fifty thousand returned to share in this "glorious" restoration, a very small number compared to the million or more persons who came with Moses out of Egypt. The older ones who could remember the glories of Solomon's temple structure broke down in tears when they saw the humble foundation of the restored temple (Ezra 3:12). This could not be paradise!

No, it could not.

But the return to "the land" and the rebuilding of the temple point the way. These events depict not merely return but rejuvenation, resurrection from the dead, anticipating the total restoration of God's people.

Five hundred years before the coming of Christ, the prophets of this restoration period spoke with prophetic anticipation of the blessings coming on their land. Jerusalem would be a city without walls, yet a wall of fire would surround it (Zech. 2:4–5). The glory of this tiny temple would be greater than Solomon's grand structure, and the wealth of all nations would flow to it (Hag. 2:9).

All this hyperbolic language—what could it mean?

It meant that God had something better. Circumstances better than the best that could be imagined under the current limitations of the cosmos would characterize the blessings of the future. The promise of the land would be fulfilled by nothing less than a restored paradise. As Isaiah had predicted earlier, the wolf would lie down with the lamb, and a little child would lead them (Isa. 11:6). No more would sin and sorrow reign, nor thorns infest the ground.

When the Christ actually came, the biblical perspective on the "land" experienced radical revision. Observing how the Jewish leadership and Herod treated John the Baptist, Jesus strategically launched his own ministry in Galilee of the Gentiles, at Capernaum, which was "by the sea" (Matt. 4:12–16; cf. Isa. 9:1–2). It was not without reason that the Lord had indicated to Abraham that he must settle on this narrow strip of land that joined three continents. For thousands of years travelers from Africa to Europe, from Asia to Africa passed along the *via maris*, the "way of the sea" (see Map 1). Right by the locale of Capernaum they passed, and they continued to pass by throughout the days of Jesus. By inaugurating his public ministry in Galilee of the Gentiles along the major international trade route, Jesus was making a statement. This land would serve as a springboard to all nations. The kingdom of God encompassed a realm that extended well beyond the borders of ancient Israel. As Paul so pointedly indicates, Abraham's promise from a new covenant perspective meant that he would be heir of the cosmos (Rom. 4:13). All nations, lands, and peoples would experience the blessings of this benevolent rule.

The radical implications of Jesus' pointing his ministry toward the whole of the world rather than confining himself to the land of Canaan need to be appreciated fully. By setting this perspective on his ministry, Jesus cleared the way for the

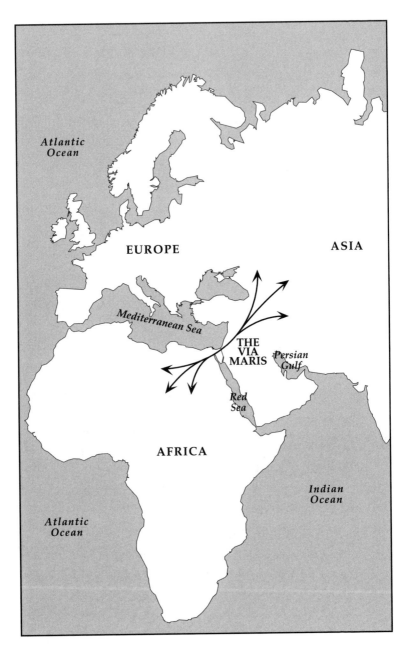

Map 1. The Land as a Bridge Connecting Three Continents

old covenant "type" to be replaced by the new covenant "antitype." The imagery of return to a "land" flowing with milk and honey was refocused on a rejuvenation that would embrace the whole of God's created order. It was not just Canaan that would benefit in the establishment of the kingdom of the Messiah. The whole cosmos would rejoice in the renewal brought about by this newness of life.

CHAPTER TWO

THE LAND FROM
WEST TO EAST

The prevailing weather patterns of this Middle Eastern land travel from west to east. Beginning over the Mediterranean Sea, winds, clouds, and rains first cross the coastal plains of Philistia. Then they ascend to traverse the rolling hills of the Shephelah and the Judean mountains of the middle section of the land. Next comes the deep rift of the Jordan depression, and finally the Transjordan highlands of ancient Edom and Moab. Once more, the compactness of this territory should be kept in mind. Crossing this land from west to east does not involve a long trek similar to a transcontinental trip from California to Maine, or from France to Russia. The girth of this, the most significant land in the history of the world, is no more than eighty miles across as the traveler journeys from the Mediterranean coast through Jerusalem to the Transjordan desert.

The Mediterranean Coast

The distant *coasts and islands of the Mediterranean* were to the people of Palestine the "ends of the earth" (see Map 2). This great sea gets its name from its situation in the "middle of the lands," and these realms were to the peoples of biblical times the outer edges of the world as they knew it.

So the prophetic vision of a worldwide expansion of faith in the one true living God and Redeemer of a sinful humanity is described in terms of reaching to the distant isles (Isa. 42:4). When Jonah determines to flee to Tarshish, he sets his sights on the Iberian Peninsula (modern-day Spain and Portugal), the outer limits of the world as he knew it. Ironically, in attempting to keep the gospel of repentance and faith from the heathen Ninevites as a way of protecting the favored position of Israel, Jonah became God's instrument of spreading the good news to the "ends of the earth" through the on-board conversion of the heathen sailors as they made their way to Tarshish.

The apostle Paul as God's chosen emissary to the nations set himself with determination to reach the same goal as Jonah (Rom. 1:10, 13; 15:23–24). He expected to "pass through" the capitol city of the world. But he didn't worry in the least about hurting the feelings of the Romans when he indicated that his goal was not their great city, for he must fulfill God's purpose by taking the Gospel to the "ends of the earth." Once more it becomes obvious that God had a definite purpose in view when he carefully chose this narrow landbridge called Canaan that connects three continents. Abraham had to leave Ur in Chaldea and go to this other land long before he knew it would be bordered by the Mediterranean Sea because God intended that the descendants of the chosen Patriarch transmit the blessings of redemption to all the nations of the world.

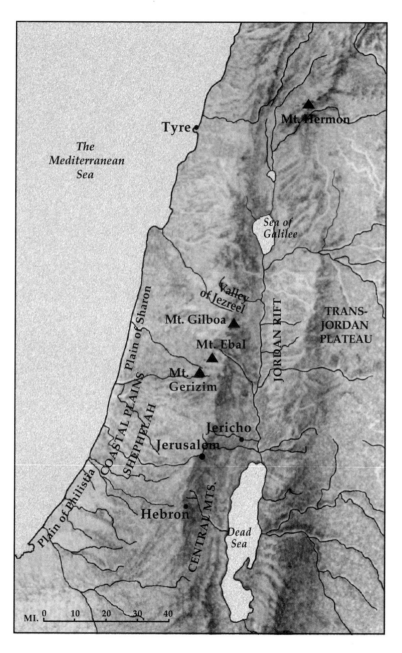

Map 2. The Land from West to East

The Plains of Philistia and Sharon

The *coastal plains* of Philistia and Sharon have no natural deep-water ports to establish this area as a world-class trading center. Shallow, sandy beaches characterize the western edge of the land of the Bible rather than the inlets and ports of places such as Greece and Italy. Here and there in such cities as Ashkelon, Joppa, Dor, and Acco, enough depth of water exists for ships to come and go. The Phoenicians and the inhabitants of Tyre to the north became adept at trading by water. But the Israelites never became known for their seaworthy achievements. Solomon instituted significant trade by sea, but his activity was funneled mainly through the port of Elath, located far south and east of the Mediterranean. There is indeed the case of good King Jehoshaphat who made a bad alliance with wicked King Amaziah of Israel. The results were a tragic shipwreck of Israel's efforts to "subdue the earth" by way of the sea (cf. 2 Chron. 20:35–37). To a large extent, the coastal plain remained an unpossessed realm in Israel's developments, even though the psalmist stood in awe of those that go down to the sea in ships, beholding the wonders of the deep (Ps. 107:23–24).

The Rolling Hills

Within twelve miles of the Philistine coast traveling eastward come the *rolling hills* known as the *Shephelah*. These pleasant hills and dales form naturally broad valleys that open up the interior of the land. As a consequence, this territory always has been militarily significant as the first line of defense for Jerusalem and its environs. As armies have tromped along the flatlands of the coast headed from Europe and Asia toward Egypt and Africa, they invariably have headed upward into these valleys as the way of easiest access to the capitol of the land. The Shephelah thus became the place for pitched battles between the Israelites and their aggressive enemies. In one of these valleys, Samson took his stand against the Philistine host with the jawbone of an ass (Judg. 14, 15). In another, little David and giant Goliath had their famous showdown as their respective armies looked on (1 Sam. 17). In still another of these valleys, the dark-bearded Assyrian named Sennacherib laid siege to the last garrison of Israel at Lachish and sent his emissaries to Jerusalem, demanding their unconditional surrender (2 Kings 18:17–26). The strategic location of these valleys as ways of access to the heartland of the country explains the significance of the bridal gift of Gezer, a fortified city in the Shephelah, to Solomon by the king of Egypt (1 Kings 9:16). By this action, the glory of Israel's anointed king, their "messiah," is seen in the virtual abdication of any possibility of military assault by a nation as powerful as Egypt. Even though this concession was clouded by Solomon's politically motivated marriage to the foreign daughter of the pharaoh, the expanding glory of the Israelite monarch became obvious. Otherwise the king of Egypt never would have considered establishing such an unbreakable truce with his previously insignificant neighbor to the north.

The Central Mountains

After the rolling hills of the Shephelah come the *central mountains* of the land. Rising quickly from sea level at the Mediterranean to an elevation of some 2,400 feet at Jerusalem, this mountainous backbone runs south to north roughly a distance of ninety miles. This central range connects Hebron in the south of Judea with the peaks of Gerizim and Ebal in Samaria, and continues on to Mount Gilboa on the southern edge of the Jezreel plain in Galilee. It is in the out-of-the-way hills of Judean territory that the most significant events of the world's history have occurred. In a narrow space of approximately twenty square miles, God's work of redemption that has set the course of the history of the world had its initial beginnings and its consummate realizations. The first offerings of Abraham as he entered the land and the last offering of himself by Jesus Christ occurred in this region of relative obscurity.

Is it not just like the God of the Bible to choose this particular place to stage the most momentous events of the world's history? All roads of the world do not naturally lead to this hallowed place. As a matter of fact, the well-traveled paths of the region completely bypass this central territory of the land of the Bible. Indeed, the roadway called the "patriarchal highway" winds along the mountainous ridge running through this area. But the main international thoroughfares follow the flatlands of the coast and the eastern edge of Transjordan. To end up in this territory, a person must first set his mind to go there. Even today, Jerusalem cannot boast an international airport. Lesser-known Tel Aviv must serve as first host to the multitude of pilgrims deplaning today in the land of the Bible.

In this central hill country, Abraham and Sarah received confirmation of the promises concerning their land, their seed, and their destiny of being a blessing to the world (Gen. 12:6–7). Into this same region, Joshua came to confirm the covenant at the precise place that had been indicated earlier to Moses by the Lord (Deut. 11:29–30; 27:12–13; Josh. 8:30–35). It was also along this same central ridge that David was anointed and began his rule in the highlands of Hebron (2 Sam. 2:1–4). In this region Solomon built his glorious temple to the Lord, and in the same locale Zerubbabel supervised its modest restoration after the devastations of the exile. In the southern hills of Judea, the Virgin gave birth to the incarnate Son of God at Bethlehem; and in the nearby hills of Jerusalem, he returned to climax his ministry on earth. Jesus did not sojourn to Athens, Rome, or Cairo to perform his last saving, sacrificial act. Instead he came back to within seven miles of the place where he had been born. In these same mountains and on the road to nearby Emmaus, he first showed himself as the Victor over the last enemy of his people. Here also he ascended in glory to the Father, and from his exalted position in heaven he poured out the life-restoring Holy Spirit on his disciples assembled here.

There is no other place on earth like it. Compacted into a space that can be walked in a day, the most significant events of God's working in the world have occurred. Here is the place that people can study until they come to appreciate something of the wonder of God's working in the world.

The Jordan Rift

But no less wondrous, at least as a topological phenomenon, is the next section of the country as the traveler continues toward the east. Less than twenty miles from Jerusalem is the *Jordan River rift*. Far to the north the melting snows of Mount Hermon contribute to the waters that rush through Lake Huleh and the Sea of Galilee, down the rolling Jordan as it twists and turns, doubling back almost to meet itself until it empties all its accumulated deposits into the Dead Sea, the lowest point on the surface of the earth. In a mere one hundred miles, the terrain drops dramatically from 9,200 feet above sea level at the peak of Mount Hermon to 1,300 feet below sea level at the surface of the Dead Sea. This same deep geological rift continues downward along the eastern half of Africa, forming lakes, rivers, and valleys as it goes.

The Jordan! How many stories, songs, and myths surround this ambulating stream! No doubt it has been sung about, prayed about, and preached about in more languages and dialects than any other river of the world.

> *Dat River Jordan,*
> *So chilly and cold.*
> *It chills de body,*
> *But not de soul.*

Because the land of Canaan as the image of eternal rest lies on its "other" side, the chilly waters of the Jordan have rolled through history as symbolic divider between this world and

that which is to come. But this great river has enough significance in Scripture itself apart from the inevitable accretions
of the ages. Here Joshua directed that the feet of the priests
step into its flooded waters to clear the way for the Israelite
nation to pass over dry-shod (Josh. 3). At the fords of this
river the Israelite warriors applied the test of the "shibboleth,"
and from the jungle of the Jordan came the imagery of the
rugged challenge the prophet of the Lord must face (Judg.
12:4–6; Jer. 12:5–6). Here also John the Baptist first preached
the gospel of repentance for the forgiveness of sins, and with its
waters he baptized the One whose sandals he did not regard
himself as worthy to unloose (Matt. 3:13–17; John 1:27).
Hermon, whose melting snows serve among its sources, is the
most likely location of the Lord's transfiguration, the lake of
Galilee a prominent place of his ministry and miracles. On
his last, long journey to Jerusalem, Jesus crossed over the Jordan
and then back again to fulfill his mission of preaching and
teaching. As a final stop before plunging into the tumultuous
events of the last week of his life, he paused in the Jordan valley
at Jericho long enough to give sight to blind Bartemaeus and
transform the life of little Zacchaeus.

At the end of the river's meandering pathway lies the
Dead Sea, an amazing geological phenomenon in itself. As
though it were not noteworthy enough that the surface of
this sea is 1,300 feet below sea level, the northern half of its
waters plunge to a bottom situated another 1,300 feet below
its surface. The waters of this sea have no outlet, and by
processes of evaporation have become so salty that hardly any
living thing can survive. Around its shallow southern end may
be found a number of strangely configured rock formations,
which some have proposed to be the ancient memorial of Lot's
wife, who was united by her own affections with the cities of
Sodom and Gomorrah in their destruction (Gen. 19:23–26).
The site of these ancient cities may be located in this very region. But their memory is preserved more lastingly through the
Lord's warning: The person who forgets his pointed admoni-

tion to "remember Lot's wife" may suffer a similar fate when the circumstances that led to their doom return (Luke 17:28–32).

Sharply rising slopes ascend from the western bank of the Dead Sea toward the Judean wilderness, forming deep canyons dotted with occasional springs. Here David hid from maddened King Saul at En Gedi, waiting for the Lord to take action in confirming his role as anointed ruler of Israel (1 Sam. 24). Here also, a thousand years later, the devotees of Qumran situated themselves so they could wait for the messiah they hoped would lead them out of the wilderness into a purified Jerusalem. Along the eastern shores of this same sea, the rocky terrain rises even more dramatically to form the peaks of Transjordan, which is the last section of the Bible's land as the traveler moves from west to east.

The Transjordan

The name *Transjordan* derives from a perspective that looks eastward from the western banks of the Jordan. Moses spoke of the territories of Ammon and Moab as the land "across the Jordan" (*"trans-*Jordan") even though he personally never viewed the land from that perspective. For he lived in the certainty that God would give them the land he had promised. All future generations of Israelites viewed this territory as "beyond the Jordan" or "Transjordan."

Israel made its approach to the Land of Promise through Transjordan because the people had lacked the faith forty years earlier to claim their allotted inheritance. Yet as a consequence of this rerouting, the people were introduced to the high plateaus of Edom and Moab, as well as the rich pasturelands of Gilead and Bashan. Some of this territory eventually was claimed as the land of their allotment by Reuben, Gad, and half the tribe of Manasseh.

The descendants of Edom, Moab, and Ammon were related to Abraham's seed through the line of Esau and by the incestuous actions of Abraham's nephew Lot with his own daughters (Gen. 19:36–38). Throughout Israelite history, these people continually harassed God's people. But in the end, God's grace prevailed even in this confused situation. Ruth, of Moabite descent, became the matriarch of David's honored ancestors, and eventually was included in the line of the Lord Jesus (Ruth 4:13–17; Matt. 1:5). Amos prophesied about the day in which the Transjordan Edomites would share equally as the chosen people of God. Though "Gentiles," they would bear the name of the Lord, dwelling in the restored tent of David (Amos 9:11–12). This prophetic anticipation of the inclusion of the long-term enemies of God's people found its historical realization in the outpouring of the Holy Spirit on the Gentiles without their ever having become Jews (Acts 15:12–18). God's outpouring of his greatest blessing on these people who had stood through the ages against the people of God symbolically displayed the Lord's intent to bless all the peoples of the world through the descendants of Abraham. For if Esau and Moab can become heirs of God's redemptive promises, then peoples of all other nations of the earth surely can be included.

Traveling across the Land of Promise from west to east can provide many insights into the purposes of God for the whole of the world. In microcosmic fashion the design of the land serves as a means of embodying the truth of God intended for all nations. Similar insights may be gained by an overview of the land based on a journey from south to north.

CHAPTER THREE

THE LAND FROM
SOUTH TO NORTH

Scanning the land from a different perspective can provide new insight into the significance of its various features for the plans and the purposes of God. Yet since the land is the same, this second perspective should complement the previous overview. So now consider the land of the Bible by moving from the south toward its northern borders (see Map 3).

Egypt

Outside the land but integral to its history is *Egypt,* the place of Israel's national beginnings. Before the patriarchal descent into this region, God told Abraham what to expect. For four

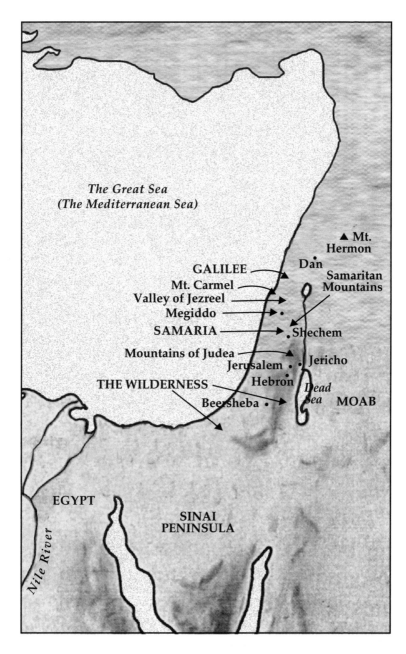

The Great Sea
(The Mediterranean Sea)

▲ Mt. Hermon

Dan

GALILEE

Samaritan Mountains

Mt. Carmel

Valley of Jezreel

Megiddo

SAMARIA

Shechem

Mountains of Judea

Jericho

Jerusalem

THE WILDERNESS

Hebron

Dead Sea

MOAB

Beersheba

EGYPT

SINAI PENINSULA

Nile River

Map 3. The Land from South to North

hundred years, his descendants would suffer oppression under alien hands while the Lord showed his patience toward the degenerating Canaanite population (Gen. 15:13, 16). As the time of release drew near, the Egyptian pharaoh's actions took on devilish proportions. His lying wonders, his murder of the infants, his prideful and unyielding stubbornness toward the good purposes of God revealed him to be the tool of Satan, God's age-old adversary. But severely beaten through repeated plagues and then struck by the death angel sent from God, Pharaoh relented long enough to let God's people go. His repentence proved insincere as his army pursued Israel to the brink of the sea, only to be answered by a final humbling under vengeful waves.

The judgment of God on Egypt and his favor toward Israel cannot and must not be interpreted as a fixed discrimination along ethnic, national, or territorial lines. For the positions of priority and rejection can change all too quickly. Egypt, as a leading nation in Africa, has not been confined to a state of banishment from the blessings of God; and neither has Israel been confirmed perpetually in a position of assured blessing. If that were the case, what does the marriage of Moses to a Cushite woman mean (Num. 12:1)? How then could the prophecy of Isaiah be understood when he boldly declares that in response to the cry of the Egyptians, the covenant LORD will send them a "savior and defender"; and the Lord Almighty will pronounce, "Blessed be Egypt my people" (Isa. 19:19–20, 25)? What then would be the meaning of the total reversal of circumstances when the land of Egypt provided a safe place for the Christ child while Herod the half-Jew sought to take his life (Matt. 2:13–15)? What then would be meant by the Lord's snatching Philip out of the midst of a revival among the Samaritans and sending him out in the desert to minister Christ and his baptism to an Ethiopian returning to Africa (Acts 8:5–7, 26–39)? These developments must mean that Egypt and Africa as a nation and a territory cannot stand second-rate in God's purposes of redemption. They too may become heirs of all God's covenant promises, a blessing in the earth.

But at the dawn of redemption's workings, Egypt served as the satanic oppressor of God's people. That land, its nation, and its people stood as the symbol of the seed of Satan among the descendants of womankind.

The Wilderness

Next in the movement from south to north comes *the wilderness*. Through all the ages, the desert has represented the place of testing and trial for God's people. During their wilderness wandering, the lack of bread and water meant that Israel must keep trusting God even when deprived of sustenance for life. When the miraculous supply of bread from heaven came regularly, the people were tempted to lust for more and complain about so little. But only by submissive trust under adverse circumstances could they learn the lesson of the desert: "Man does not live on bread alone but on every word that comes from the mouth of the Lord" (Deut. 8:3).

But even forty years in the school of the desert was not enough. As soon as they prospered in the land flowing with milk and honey, Israel forgot the lessons of their long years in the wilderness. The allurements of the Canaanite culture captured them; and they did their homage to the Baal-gods of materialism, even to the point of yielding their infant children to the sacrificial fires. So they had need once more for the stripping down brought about by the desert. Hosea the prophet predicted it. God the Almighty would play the part of a paramour, lure them into the wilderness, and there leave them stripped of their material comforts until they found their way in repentance once more. Before they received any further blessings from him, the scorching desert, the place of scorpions and snakes, of thorns and thistles would do its humbling work (cf. Hos. 2:2–3; 8–10).

So it should not have caught God's people by surprise when the rough and ruddy messenger of the new covenant should take his stand "in the wilderness." A sin-softened nation must come to him in the desert and submit to a baptismal washing of soul-searching repentance for the forgiveness of sins (Matt. 3:1–6). Surrounded by the rugged terrain of desert sand and barren rock, the Israel of the new covenant should be reminded of their ancient experience in the same environment, and turn from their attachment to self-gratifying things that displaced the love of their God.

Neither should it be surprising that the Son of God himself met the Devil in the desert. Though forty days is not forty years, the similarity of numbers and circumstance is enough to connect the two incidents. Tempted over bread, power, and priorities—as was the Israel of old—God's true Son succeeded where the old Israel failed the test. After a forty-day fast, he would not yield to the temptation of turning desert stones into loaves of bread. For he believed that even the word of God that deprives of sustenance is actually a source of true life (Matt. 4:1–11).

The role of the desert in the experience of God's people returns as a constant factor of significance. Even today, God's people must learn the lessons of the wilderness. Every new generation made alive by God's grace may be characterized as a people of the wilderness undergoing a prolonged time of testing after exodus as they travel toward the rest that remains for the people of God (Heb. 3:7–4:11).

The Mountains of Judea

The traveler's rest is ahead, for next come the southern *mountains of Judea*. It was up into these mountains that the weary Israelites sent their twelve spies, representing the twelve tribes of Israel. There they found the land "flowing with milk and honey"—not literally, but by way of contrast with Egypt and the desert they were so anxious to forget. Back from this region the spies came, laden with a cluster of grapes larger than a single man could carry. But their lack of faith kept them from claiming the superabundance of God's blessing (Num. 14:1–4). Their presumption in going up after the Lord had denied them entry brought their defeat by the inhabitants of the land (Deut. 1:41–46). They went up into the high hill country and were beaten back by their enemies. So for another thirty-eight years they wandered in the desert, barred from enjoyment of the "paradise" of God.

These pictures of a land resembling "paradise" must not be taken too literally. The mountains and valleys of Judea have a beauty all their own, but they are by no means excessively productive. One Jewish fable supposes that at Creation, God divided between two large storks all the stones to be scattered over the surface of the earth. But the sack of one of the giant birds broke over Palestine, so that half the stones of the world tumbled onto the land of the Bible. Fields of grain and productive vineyards may be found in parts of the Judean territory. But only by poetic imagery may this land be equated with "paradise."

As in most matters related to the geography of this land, it is necessary to think in categories that are smaller than first may be imagined. The territory of Judea stretches northward from the town of Beersheba on the edge of the desert in the south for a distance of only fifty miles to the region of Jerusalem. Calculating Judah's territory from west to east, the distance from the Judean mountains to the Dead Sea is a distance of only about eighteen miles. Yet this small region encompasses all the area assigned by lot to the most significant tribe of the twelve. Even before the land division in Joshua's day, it had been predicted that the promised ruler for Israel would come from Judah's tribe (Gen. 49:10). Eventually David was born in Bethlehem, seven miles south of Jerusalem. He first set up his throne in high Hebron, ten miles south of his birthplace. From this vantage point, David could look eastward across the Dead Sea to the mountains of Moab, and in the opposite direction to the shores of the Mediterranean. The young king could almost see the Philistine troops training for their next assault against his people.

Judean land divides principally into two basic regions. Follow the north-south spinal ridge of mountains connecting Hebron with Jerusalem, and the territory splits naturally into two segments according to the pattern of rainfall that comes from the Mediterranean. As clouds move eastward, they are forced upward by the Judean mountain peaks, condense in the higher, cooler atmosphere, and release their moisture on Judah's western slopes. Once they have topped this range of mountains, the clouds descend again to drift over the Dead Sea fault, only to be urged upward once more by the even higher mountains of Moab in Transjordan. But as a result of this centuries-old weather pattern, cultivated lands characterize the western portion of Judah, while desert descends into the Jordan fault on the eastern slopes of this same mountain range. The Hebron-Bethlehem-Jerusalem complex straddles this range, having widely divergent terrains on alternate sides. As a consequence, David and his descendants knew firsthand the barren abandonments associated with a parched and barren land, as well as the exuberant delights springing from a well-watered garden. Move westward and they experienced one extreme; turn to the east and they witnessed exactly the opposite circumstance.

In these Judean hills, King David learned the lessons of the "good shepherd." Hours at this occupation used fruitfully in meditation may have provided the raw material that inspired David's most famous composition: "The Lord is my shepherd; I shall not want" (Ps. 23:1 NKJV). These experiences also established in the mind of the young king the proper pattern of a god-like ruler who "shepherded [his people] according to the integrity of his heart, and guided them by the skillfulness of his hands" (Ps. 78:72 NKJV).

Along the outskirts of Judea, David learned the lessons of patience through adversity as he waited for the fulfillment of God's promises to him. Saul relentlessly sought him in caves, around the base of mountains, through villages, and into the desert. But David refused to lift a hand in self-defense by touching the Lord's anointed. He chose instead to trust the timing of the Lord. Eventually David learned all the lessons taught by the land. As one who patiently humbled himself before his God, he was in due time exalted above all his enemies.

Samaria

Located north of Jerusalem is the territory of *Samaria,* with its capitol complex at Shechem and the city of Samaria. Situated at the foot of the twin mountains of Gerizim and Ebal was the first altar to the Lord built in the land. At this specific place the God who had called Abraham out of Ur of the Chaldees finally indicated that this was the land that would belong to him and his descendants forever (Gen. 12:6–7). To this place, God commanded Israel to return and assemble for the reading of the curses and the blessings of the covenant (Deut. 11:29–30). Joshua later led the people directly to this locale so they could fulfill the Lord's command in renewing the covenant (Josh. 8:30–35).

It was a sad day years later when a rival capitol to the Lord's designated city of Jerusalem was set up in this same region. Samaria became the center for a series of self-willed dynasties in the northern kingdom, while the single dynasty of David continued in Jerusalem as the only legitimate throne of Israel. Yet the Lord in his longsuffering did not absolutely abandon the ten tribes of the north. Located in the heart of the territory assigned to the descendants of Joseph, Samaria continued to be favored with the presence of God's prophets such as Elijah, Elisha, Amos, and Hosea.

But eventually the forces of Assyria made this territory taste the bitter fruit of its rebellion. Slow starvation in the once-prosperous city of Samaria led women to feed on their own offspring (2 Kings 6:26–29). Yet God encouraged them to look beyond their unthinkable tragedies and hope in a *Messiah ben Ephraim,* the Son of God's right hand who would return the hearts of Ephraim and Manasseh to their Lord (Gen. 49:22–26; Ps. 80:14–19).

The remnant of Samaria that survived the Assyrian invasion eventually became the despised of the land, for the conquering king of Assyria repopulated this territory with foreign peoples who mixed in marriage with the people of God (2 Kings 17:24). The tradition of a rival center of power and worship continued into the times of the new covenant, so that the Jews of Jesus' day insisted on having no dealings with the Samaritans (John 4:9).

But the coming of Jesus Christ struck at the foundations of this prejudicial presumption. He drank water from the well at Shechem drawn by a sinful Samaritan woman. In exchange he gave her a drink of the waters of eternal life, found in the forgiveness offered freely to sinful outcasts. He told the Jews the parable of the "good Samaritan" who was the only one to offer the hand of help to a wounded traveler going down to Jericho from Jerusalem. Despite the fact that Samaritan villages rejected him because he had set his face toward Jerusalem, the exalted Lord poured out his Holy Spirit on the Samaritans just as he had done for the Jerusalemites (Acts 8:4–25).

Does not every age and community have its "Samaritans," those nearby neighbors of different class, custom, language, race, or nationality? Are there not near us all the equivalent of lower castes, inner-city dwellers, or religious exclusivists? Is not the commission of Christ the same for us as for the first apostles—that we go to our Samaria as well as to our Jerusalem?

Galilee

Then there is *Galilee,* the land of the Gentiles. Last in the land as the traveler moves from south to north is the territory of the vast hordes of various nationalities representing all the peoples of the world. In this region, the people of God found themselves constantly in contact with the rest of humanity. They could not have escaped this interchange if they had wished. Whether they were in a period of national strength or weakness made no difference. Either traveling warriors or itinerant merchants wound their way through Galilee of the Gentiles. For God had so ordained it by the very way in which he shaped the continents. This narrow strip of land alone connected the three continental masses from which human civilization emerged. Africa hung as though from a thread, with Europe and Asia balanced above. All the land traffic of these three continents eventually made their interchanges by way of Galilee of the Gentiles. It was by the strategic location of this place for his people that the Lord intended eventually to reach the world with the Gospel that was the power of God unto salvation, to the Jew first and also to the Gentile.

Slopes descending from the mountains of Samaria connect Galilee with the rest of Palestine. Intermittent passes open this northern territory to the flat coastal plains along the Mediterranean that lead to Egypt and the rest of North Africa. Prominent among these passes was the one guarded by the fortress city of Megiddo, always ready to stand against advancing armies. At this place Josiah, the last good king of Judah, perished at the hands of Pharaoh Necho of Egypt. Josiah's presumption led him to ignore the Lord's warning, but his death stirred Jeremiah to compose a prophetic lament (2 Chron. 35:25). The occurrence of this tragic event at this strategic place took on apocalyptic significance with the prophecies of the last great battle of Armageddon, which name includes an allusion to ancient Megiddo (cf. Zech. 12:10–11; Rev. 16:16). An excessive literalism not suitable to the pattern of Scripture's own self-interpretation has led some Christians today to anticipate an actual confrontation of the armies of God with the forces of Satan, using tanks, guns, and jet warplanes at the site of ancient Megiddo. But the warfare of these last days has been clearly described by the apostle Paul as not being with flesh and blood but with spiritual powers that must be overcome by the weapons of prayer and the sword of the Spirit, which is the Word of God (Eph. 6:10–18). Insofar as the final conflict is concerned, Scripture indicates that when the Lord appears in glory, he shall slay all his enemies with the breath of his mouth (2 Thess. 2:8). In this sense, the symbolism of this place called Megiddo, now immortalized in Scripture as Armageddon, cannot be overlooked. Christ shall return in glory to devastate all his and our enemies.

A second prominent feature of Galilee's terrain are the broad plains running west to east on a slight diagonal from the Mediterranean to the Jordan River. Broken here and there with mountains, such as Gilboa where Saul fell and Tabor where Deborah assembled her troops, these broad expanses known as Jezreel (or Esdraelon) provided fertile soil for crops to grow and ample space for chariots to maneuver. So Sisera bullied Israel with his nine hundred iron chariots, capable of racing across the broad valleys of Galilee, until the Lord raised up Deborah to deliver his people (Judg. 4:12–16). So also the Midianites swarmed across these same broad expanses, robbing Israel of its rich grain as soon as it could be harvested, until the Lord commissioned the mighty man Gideon (Judg. 6:1–6; 11–14). In this same territory, the Philistine hordes spread their troops to do battle with Israel until Saul and Jonathan tragically fell on the slopes of Mount Gilboa (1 Sam. 31:1–6).

Across these plains marched the Assyrian armies of Sennacherib and the Babylonian troops of Nebuchadnezzar. The Medo-Persian, the Greek, the Roman, and the Crusader armies each in their turn trudged over this same soil. In more recent history, the British forces under General Allenby fought a strategic battle in the twentieth century.

But more significant than all these goings and comings of rising and falling nations was the strategic role of this same Galilee of the Gentiles in the spread of the Gospel of God to all the nations of the world. When Jesus heard that John the Baptist had been arrested by Herod Antipas, king of the Jews, he left Nazareth and went to Capernaum, which is located by the sea (Matt. 4:12–15). Both Nazareth and Capernaum are located in Galilee, but Capernaum is more significant as a point of passage for countless peoples traveling between the continents. Seeing how the ruler of the Jewish nation responded to his official forerunner, Jesus opened his public ministry by deliberately situating himself at Capernaum so he could reach out to touch all nations with his Gospel. At this locale he could preach to all the peoples of the world—not simply to the Jews—about the worldwide "kingdom of heaven" that was near (Matt. 4:17).

The gospel writer makes the point that Jesus deliberately launched his ministry by "the way to the sea" in "Galilee of the Gentiles" for the purpose of fulfilling prophecy (Matt. 4:14–15). Throughout the ages, it had been God's plan to reach all the nations of the world with the saving Gospel of his Son. This intent found fulfillment throughout Jesus' ministry. He went continually throughout all the villages of Galilee preaching the Good News (Matt. 4:23). Capernaum continued to be the central point of his ministry as he made use of Lake Galilee to reach out to the various cities and villages. After his resurrection, he delivered his Great Commission to his disciples in the region of Galilee of the Gentiles (Matt. 28:16–20). From that point until today, his Gospel has spread among all the nations of the world. In this sense, Galilee continues to have significance as a symbolic representation of the ongoing purposes of the Lord to minister his saving grace to all the peoples of the world.

Still farther toward the northernmost point of Canaan was the location of the second settlement of the tribe of Dan. Not finding the peace they desired in their original allotment of land at the edge of Philistine territory, the tribe of Dan went to the nation's northern edge seeking a new home. When they came to the town of Laish, they noted that the people were "living in safety . . . unsuspecting and secure" (Judg. 18:7). They attacked these peace-loving inhabitants in an unprovoked act of aggression, thinking that in this region they would find the peace they desired so earnestly. Little did they realize that they were settling directly in the pathway of all the marching armies that would tromp across the land bridge of Palestine. In this fool's paradise of their own making, they would find no peace at all. To the contrary, they would face a continual stream of armed aggressors, warriors aspiring to conquer the world.

To this point, a journey has been made from Beersheba to Dan, and from the Mediterranean to the Jordan River and beyond. Virtually every form of earth's varied terrain is packed into this small territory, and each section of this land is crowded with remembrances of God's way of working redemption in the world. The whole of the land was designed by the Lord for his good purposes as he determined them before the foundation of the world.

PART TWO

SPECIFICS
OF THE LAND

The land of the Bible in its larger dimensions clearly was designed by the Lord for the purpose of embodying redemptive truth. All its dominant characteristics serve as large pieces of a puzzle whose interconnection makes the truth of God forever more memorable. Its location in joining three continents, its proximity to the desert and the sea, its varying regions all make their distinctive contribution toward emphasizing redemptive truth.

The same purpose of the Lord finds more explicit manifestation in the specifics of the land. Details of the geography, topography, and demographics of this specific place all contribute to making vivid the redemptive purposes of God respecting this fallen world. So now observe the particulars of the land in terms of mountains and rivers, climate and vegetation, towns and cities.

CHAPTER FOUR

MOUNTAINS AND RIVERS

Mountains

The major mountain ranges of the land all run basically in a north-south direction, and are three: the Judean hills, the mountains of Samaria, and the Transjordan plateau. The Lebanon and Anti-Lebanon ranges are situated in the northwestern section of the land but essentially are out of the area where most of the events of the Bible occurred.

The hills of Judea rise quickly from the desert area of the Sinai peninsula and reach a height of about three thousand feet above sea level. As indicated earlier, the ridge of the Judean range provides the line of demarcation between cultivated lands sloping westward toward the Mediterranean and arid desert descending rapidly to the Dead Sea. The principal cities of this region are Hebron, Bethlehem, and Jerusalem.

The Samaritan mountains shape the central region of the country, running north from Bethel to the plains of Esdraelon (Jezreel) in Galilee (see Map 4). Since these mountains do not reach the elevation of the Judean hills, the rainfall is more evenly distributed across Samaria. In addition, broader valleys that produce crops more easily are interspersed throughout the area. Principal cities include Bethel, Shiloh, Shechem, and Samaria.

The Transjordan range reaches as high as five thousand feet. It begins in the south with the peaks of Edom and runs north through Moab, the territory of Ammon, Gilead, and Bashan. Significant among its cities are the rock-carved fortress of Petra, the modern city of Amman (site of ancient Rabbah), and Ramoth-Gilead to the north. Once more the pattern prevails of rains along the western slopes, which disappear as the weather patterns reach the vast expanses of the Arabian desert that emerges quickly to the east.

These mountainous ranges, compacted into the small region of Palestine, contribute greatly to the variety of the terrain. They provide lines of demarcation that quickly create realms of sharply contrasting geophysical characteristics.

Scattered among these various ranges are particular mountains that have played a significant part in the unfolding purposes of God. Most important is the mountain where David eventually settled his capitol city, known and beloved across the ages as Mount Zion, the designated dwelling place of the Lord.

Beautiful for elevation though it may be, this mountain is not by any means the highest peak in the area, to the surprise of many travelers. Yet its position inside a "bowl" formed by higher surrounding mountains has a number of advantages. Shaped in the form of a "V" or a "W" with its various valleys converging toward the south, two of its three sides are protected naturally from assault. Only to the north does a flattened terrain make the city vulnerable to invasion.

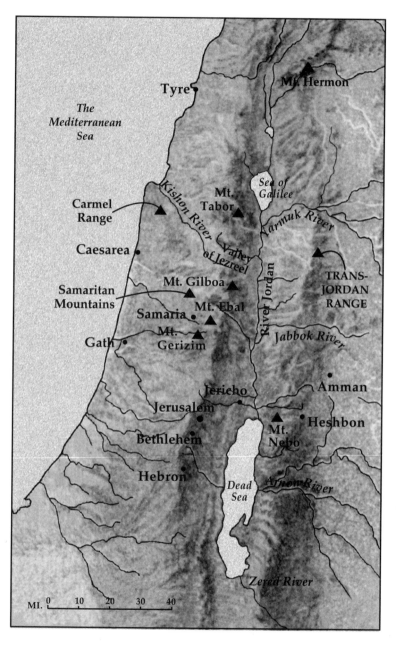

Map 4. Mountains and Rivers

43

Next in significance is the mountain of Samaria. Chosen by King Omri of the northern kingdom as the location of his capitol city, this mountain usurped the primary role that had belonged to Shechem, located less than ten miles to the southeast (1 Kings 16:23–24). Samaria stands as a rounded, isolated hill a hundred yards higher than the open vale surrounding it. Open toward the west, the mountain is situated only twenty-one miles from the Mediterranean coast. This locale no doubt must have pleased Queen Jezebel, who could look from her palace window and see the waters familiar to her as a Tyrian Baal-worshipper.

Farther toward the north along the coast is the range known as Carmel. Stretching upward from the Mediterranean Sea, this mountain was the chosen site for the contest of Elijah with the gods of Baal. Having commanded no rain for the space of three and one-half years, Elijah sent his servant to look westward from the heights of Carmel toward the sea, while the prophet prayed for the reversal of God's decree of drought. Not until the seventh time did the servant spy at a great distance a cloud as small as a man's fist rising from the waters (1 Kings 18:44). But this little cloud heralded the rapid arrival of a deluge. Having already slain the false prophets who had stood against him, the prophet now rushed down the slopes of this mighty mountain to observe the response of King Ahab and Jezebel his queen. But sad to say, the mighty wonders of the Lord worked through the prayers of his prophet only served to harden their encrusted hearts. In exhausted despair, the prophet hastened his journey deep into the territory of the south until he found rest and reassurance in the desert of Sinai (1 Kings 19:1–18).

Moving eastward from Carmel across the plain that stretches toward the Sea of Galilee, the traveler is struck by a rounded peak that stands alone. At this picturesque Mount Tabor, the Lord's people were led once more to a glorious victory. Their troops were assembled at Tabor under the leadership of Barak and Deborah. The Lord fought with them against the superior forces of Sisera, nullifying the strength of his nine hundred iron chariots with the waters of the age-old river Kishon (Judg. 5:21). When Sisera fled for his life, the wife of Heber the Kenite first filled the alien general's belly with warm milk and then pierced his temples with a tent peg (Judg. 4:18–21; 5:24–27).

Across the valley toward the south is the promontory known as Mount Gilboa, a place of true tragedy in the life of God's people. King Saul persisted in his stubborn resistance to the will of God until he and his son Jonathan lay dead on the slopes of Gilboa (1 Sam. 31:8). This disgrace was not to be told in the Philistine city of Gath. The enemies of the Lord must not be allowed to mock the Lord at the fall of his designated leaders. Let the mountains of Gilboa mourn, but let not the daughters of the uncircumcised rejoice (2 Sam. 1:20–21).

Last of the mountain peaks in Palestine to be noted is the northernmost beauty known as Hermon. Up from the Sea of Galilee some forty miles to the north, Hermon reaches a height of over nine thousand feet and remains snowcapped year-round. The Gospels indicate that it was in the region of Caesarea Philippi that Jesus' transfiguration occurred on a very high mountain (Matt. 17:1). Hermon would provide the relative seclusion necessary for such a spectacular event. So it was very likely on the slopes of Hermon, the northernmost point of Jesus' ministry, that his countenance became as brilliant as the sun in its glory (Matt. 17:2). From that point he began his "journey to Jerusalem," traveling resolutely through Galilee, Samaria, and Transjordan to his destined end (Luke 9:51–53). From the mountain of Hermon in the north to the mountain of Jerusalem in the south, he traveled with a set purpose in his heart. He would give his life for his people. He would sacrifice himself in obedience to the will of his heavenly Father to bring salvation to undeserving sinners.

Rivers

In addition to the mountains that define the terrain of Palestine are the rivers that run in the land. Though few in number, these rivers have played a prominent role in the unfolding drama of redemption.

First are the wadis of the wilderness. Strangers to the unique behavior of the wadi may be surprised at the sudden appearance or disappearance of their waters. More than one unfortunate, unsuspecting person has chosen the crevice of a dried wadi as a natural place to pitch camp or situate a sleeping bag for an overnight stay. Away from the wind and the blowing debris of the desert, the wadi's depression offers a safe shelter through the night. But in this case, appearances are deceptive. For the torrential rains that wash the distant mountains collect naturally in these dry gulches and rush into the Negev, sweeping away everything in their path. More than one stranger to this peculiar pattern has been drowned in the torrent that has rushed on him without warning.

The wadi can also serve as a positive image of God's blessings. For as streams (wadis) rush into the desert, so God's blessings come unexpectedly to refresh the weary soul (Ps. 126:4). Those who are overwhelmed with a sense of the barrenness of life can look for refreshment from the Lord at the most unsuspecting moments, just as the waters of the wadi surprise the barren wilderness.

Next come the large gorges of Transjordan that empty their periodic waters into the Dead Sea and the Jordan River. Because the western slopes of the mountain ranges receive greater amounts of rainfall, these Transjordan gullies carry much more water than the comparable wadis in Judea and Samaria.

Southernmost of the Transjordan wadis is the river Zered. This deep gorge has served traditionally as the natural division between the territory of Edom—the descendants of Esau—and the land of Moab, populated by the offspring of Lot's incestuous act with his elder daughter. It may have been in part the steep, rocky canyon of the Zered that persuaded Israel not to press on through Edomite territory when they were refused passage (Num. 20:14–21). A nation with numbers of women, children, and older people might not have survived that passage if they had been opposed by a warring community like the Edomites.

But returning thirty-eight years later, the Israelites finally crossed the Zered (Deut. 2:13–14). As a matter of fact, they even camped in its valley (Num. 21:12). This advance meant that they finally were heading toward their designated heritage assigned to them by the Lord. The crossing of this vast chasm meant that they would not turn back until the Promised Land was theirs.

On a later occasion, the Israelites had a memorable experience in the wilderness of Edom along the banks of the Zered (2 Kings 3:1–27). By reason of an entangling alliance with the northern kingdom under Joram son of Ahab, good King Jehoshaphat of Judah—along with the king of Edom—joined in a three-way alliance intended to punish Mesha, king of Moab, for refusing to pay the tribute demanded by Israel. Following their prearranged strategy, the coalition of troops circled the southern end of the Dead Sea, intending to surprise Moab by coming up suddenly out of the desert of Edom. But before they could launch their assault, they completely exhausted their supply of the most precious commodity of the desert—water. The king of Israel approached the brink of utter despair, but Jehoshaphat called for a word from the Lord through the prophet Elisha. Though he publicly scorned the vile son of Ahab, Elisha showed respect for godly King Jehoshaphat despite his obvious error of entering into an entangling alliance. The prophet predicted that without wind or rain all the ditches they could dig in the desert would be filled with water overnight. By the time of the morning sacrifice, it happened just as the prophet anticipated. Very possibly, rain had fallen in the distant hills of Edom and flooded the trenches that had just been dug.

All this time, the troops of Moab stood poised atop the cliffs of the Zered, expecting an assault from the forces of the coalition at any moment. But in the early splash of sunlight, the flooded trenches across the gorge appeared to them as blood because of its reddish tint. The Moabite army rushed across the gorge of the Zered, thinking the alliance between Edom, Israel, and Judah had gone sour. They would simply gather the spoils of an enemy that had destroyed itself. In this mentally disarmed state, the Moabites rushed into the arms of the coalition's troops. They made a hasty retreat, trying desperately to recross the Zered. But it was too late. The natural difficulties of crossing the gorge that should have been their ally now became their foil as they attempted to flee. Seeing the ruin of his nation, Mesha, king of Moab, stood on the walls of his capitol city and offered his son as a human sacrifice. The awesome sight ended the siege, and the troops of the coalition made their way back across the expanses of the Zered.

Next toward the north in Transjordan is the river Arnon, flowing into the midpoint of the eastern shore of the Dead Sea, and dividing the territory of the Moabites to the south from the Ammonites to the north. Both of these ancient peoples were relatives of Abraham, descendants of the sons born of Lot's incestuous act with his two daughters (Gen. 19:36–38). But their common ancestry did not establish a bond of brotherhood between the two nations. The topographical division created by the Arnon only accentuated their lack of unity.

The Arnon is a massive gorge two miles wide, with a depth greater than five football fields standing end on end. The main river is formed about two miles inland from the Dead Sea, where two branches join. Closer to the Arabian desert, these branches are fed by a number of tributaries, so that in Scripture it is designated by the plural, the "valleys" of the Arnon (Num. 21:14–15 RSV). These many canyons across the land create a natural border difficult to cross.

It was at the point of this crossing that Israel actually began to claim a land that would be their own. Moab had let them pass through their country peaceably. But the Amorites, who had come from across the Jordan some time earlier to claim part of the territory of the Moabites, would tolerate no passage through their territory. Led by Sihon, their king, the Amorites came with a warring horde to confront Israel as they attempted to lead their women and children across the gorges of the upper Arnon. But it was the Lord's doing, making Sihon's spirit stubborn as a way of delivering him and his territory into the hands of the Israelites (Deut. 2:30). Sihon and his forces were utterly routed. Even his capitol city of Heshbon, some twenty miles north of the Arnon gorge, became Israelite territory and later was assigned to the tribe of Reuben. From this advanced vantage point, Moses could ascend the heights of Mount Nebo paralleling the head of the Dead Sea and look across the Jordan to the land God had promised them.

Farther north, about halfway up the Jordan between the Dead Sea and the Sea of Galilee, is the Jabbok. This river also is noteworthy as a significant point of crossing in the earliest days of Israel's history. Jacob was returning to the Land of Promise after a twenty-year absence that had originated with his flight from his brother Esau who was seeking his life. Having sent gifts to his brother in Edom, Jacob learned that Esau was advancing to meet him with a troop of four hundred men. Fearing for his life, Jacob divided his two wives, eleven sons, and all his possessions into two companies. In the dark of the night these groups made their way down the steep banks of the Jabbok, crossed its waters, and prepared to present their gifts of appeasement to Jacob's estranged brother.

But Jacob remained by himself, alone on the other side of the ravine.

On that night, a messenger from God wrestled with Jacob until the break of day. This divine messenger showed his vastly superior power by crippling Jacob for life with a touch to the thigh. But the patriarch persisted in the contest, insisting that he would not release his divine opponent until the opponent had blessed him. In response to Jacob's persistence when confronted with such superior strength, the angel changed Jacob's name, indicating God's confirmation of a change of nature. His name had been Jacob, meaning "supplanter," designating a trickster who willed to overcome his adversaries by deceit. But now his name would be Israel, "prince with God." For he had struggled with both God and men, and had overcome.

By the light of the morning, a new Jacob crossed the Jabbok. He preceded the two companies and met Esau first by himself. On the banks of that ravine, the forefather of the future nation of Israel had taken on a different character. By God's grace, the true Israelite would be a transformed, new kind of person, a person who knew that his only hope in an alien world lay in the undeserved blessing of God rather than in the resourcefulness of his own cunning (cf. Gen. 32:1–32).

Last of the rivers running into the Jordan is the Yarmuk. Out of the territories of Gilead and Bashan, this river joins the Jordan just below the Sea of Galilee.

It was on the banks of the Yarmuk that Og, king of Bashan, met Israel in battle. In the ensuing struggle, Israel took all sixty of Og's fortified cities and expanded its holdings to the foot of Mount Hermon (Deut. 3:1–11). All Bashan to the north and all Gilead to the south of the Yarmuk were reckoned among Israel's most prized territories. At the time of the allotment of land to the various tribes, this area became the homeland of half the tribe of Manasseh.

So these four rivers served as natural dividers of the Transjordan territory. Though these borders were not maintained hard and fast, they basically served the purpose of drawing lines that divided the area from south to north.

The Jordan

But of course the major river of the entire region is the Jordan, dividing the land between west and east. This ancient landmark follows the deep crevice of the same fault-line that continues far into the continent of Africa, giving shape to the path of the Nile (Smith 1972, 301).

The Jordan may be envisioned as a depression with steppes, so that each lower level is narrower than the previous one. The valley in which the river flows is formed by the hills of Samaria to the west and the higher flatlands of Gilead to the east. The resulting vale varies in width from two to fourteen miles, being narrower at the northern section, then bulging and shrinking again until it finally widens as it approaches the area of Jericho near the Dead Sea. Although the river itself flows in too deep a channel to water this entire broad valley, a number of springs and brooks provide adequate moisture to keep trees and underbrush green during most of the year.

Winding, twisting, and curving back and forth on itself in this valley is a narrower depression of approximately two hundred yards to a mile in width. This depression represents the area that normally floods when the river spills over its banks, generally in the month of April. Giving the appearance from above of an "enormous green serpent" (Smith 1972, 312), this subvalley is thick with tangled brush and semitropical trees. Vividly described in Scripture as the "Pride of the Jordan," the area appropriately has been designated as a "jungle," the natural habitat in Old Testament times of lions, boars, and other wild beasts (Jer. 12:5; 49:19; 50:44).

The third level of the Jordan valley is the riverbed itself. It normally measures about ninety to one hundred feet across, and varies from three to ten feet in depth. In its descent from the southern end of the Sea of Galilee to the northernmost point of the Dead Sea, this muddy, serpentine stream clearly displays the characteristic that gave the river its name *Jordan*, which means "downward." In this straight-line distance of sixty-five miles, the river drops over two hundred yards. As it nears the end of its path, the stream descends over forty feet each mile, which causes a great rushing downward toward the Dead Sea, whose surface rests 1,300 feet below sea level, the lowest point on the earth.

And what role has this distinctive river played in the history of the land, yes, even of the world itself? There is none other like it. The crossing of this river symbolically marked the return of God's people to the lost land of paradise. It indicated the end of the days of their reproach when they had been forced to live as landless vagabonds on the earth (Josh. 5:2–9). The watery barrier to the nation's homeland could be crossed only by the powerful work of God's grace. For the Israel that stood by its flooded banks certainly was as guilty as its leader Moses, who was denied passage because of his sin. Not by reason of their faithfulness, their intelligence, or their raw might did they walk across the dry bed of the Jordan. Only because of the grace and power of the Lord, extended to an undeserving people, did they pass into the land flowing with milk and honey. Indeed, their crossing of the river took the step of faith. First the feet of the priests that carried the ark must enter the swirling floodwaters of the Jordan (Josh. 3:14–17). This sacred box borne by the priests of Israel symbolized both the throne of God on earth as well as the place where the lifeblood of the substitutionary sacrifice for sin had to be sprinkled. Only by following in faith behind this symbol of God's gracious and powerful intervention on their behalf could the people expect to see the full salvation of the Lord.

The same principle holds today. Not a single human being crosses into the realm of God's true blessing in life apart from faith in God's power and God's forgiveness. These blessings flow from the heavenly throne of grace, where Jesus Christ, who died the sinner's death despite his absolute innocence, provides pardon for deeds worthy of death done by sinners. People have never crossed through the cold waters of death and entered into the blessings of eternal life apart from their own personal appeal to the blood of Jesus Christ as a substitute for their own justly deserved banishment from the presence of an offended God. It would be good for the sophisticated, educated society of today to learn well the ancient lessons of the crossing of the Jordan. John the Baptist summoned the learned and unlearned, the high and the low to its waters for the baptism of repentance for the forgiveness of sins. This same call still goes out today.

So the Jordan has stood as a symbol of the deep rift, the unaltered barrier that exists between everyone and his or her restoration to the full blessings of the Lord. Only by God's grace and power may that barrier be crossed successfully.

CHAPTER FIVE

CLIMATE AND VEGETATION
(by John D. Currid)

The truth that the land of the Bible is a land of contrasts is doubly confirmed by a study of its climate and vegetation. Both of these factors demonstrate just how dramatic can be the contrasts in the land of the Bible.

Climate

Climate may be defined as prevailing conditions of temperature, precipitation, and air pressure in a given area. Palestine is a region of climatic transition consisting of four prominent weather zones (see Map 5).

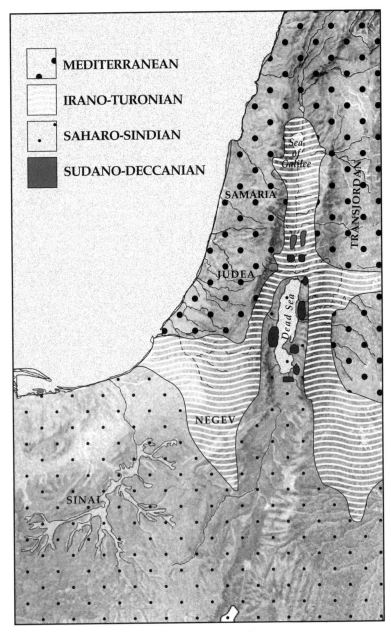

Map 5. Climate and Vegetation

1. *Mediterranean (wet zone).* This region includes the coastland and highland areas stretching from Judea to the northern parts of Palestine. Characterized as a subtropical wet zone, it averages about fourteen inches of precipitation per year. Because of its high rainfall, it is an area of many forests, with the principal trees being terebinth and evergreen oak. Most sections of the land of the Bible fall into this Mediterranean climatic zone.

2. *Irano-Turonian (dry steppe [plateau]).* Included in this zone are the Negev areas of Palestine, especially around the site of Beersheba. This region has less rainfall than the Mediterranean zone, averaging six to twelve inches per year. Lower vegetation forms survive in this area. Historically it has been characterized as a region of nomadism and simple dry farming.

3. *Saharo-Sindian (desert).* This climatic zone contains the desert areas of Palestine beginning in the southern Negev and moving further southward. It is part of a major subtropical arid zone that includes the Arabian and Saharan deserts. Only two to six inches of precipitation fall in these arid areas per year. Any farming that occurs is wholly dependent on irrigation.

4. *Sudano-Deccanian (oases).* These oasis spots appear predominantly around the shores of the Dead Sea. The areas are small, isolated climatic zones that sustain high temperatures and maintain sources of abundant sweet water. Jericho and En Gedi are prime examples of oases in the land of the Bible. The most prominent vegetation is the lotus tree.

Palestine's location within these four zones results in marked climatic variations over a small region. The distance between Jerusalem and Jericho is a scant fourteen miles, yet the climatic differences are tremendous. Jerusalem receives twenty-one inches of rain a year and has an average temperature of 64° F, while Jericho gets only six inches of precipitation and has an average temperature of 77° F. It is little wonder that King Herod the Great built a winter palace at Jericho. There he could enjoy balmy weather during the cold, rainy months of the year; yet he was never far from his main capital at Jerusalem. Suffering from paranoia over potential palace intrigue, Herod never wanted to be far from the centers of government. At Jericho, he could have both bodily comfort and governmental control.

Palestine has two well-defined seasons: a dry season in summer and a rainy season in winter. Summer is characterized by high temperatures, consistent westerly breezes, and almost drought conditions. Summer storms are a rarity. Samuel's call for a heavy thunderstorm at harvest-time underscores the infrequency of such an event (1 Sam. 12). The arid season normally begins with the penetration of the hot desert winds called *hamsin*. These winds dry up the Palestinian landscape.

The winter season in the land of the Bible is much more unpredictable. The greatest amount of precipitation falls during this season. The Bible describes this phenomenon as God's giving "the rain for your land in its season, the early and late rain" (Deut. 11:14 NASB). Precipitation may come in the form of hail or snow in the highland elevations (see Psalm 68:14). The amount of precipitation generally increases as one moves from south to north.

Climate, especially precipitation, is perhaps the most important physical factor influencing human activity in the land of the Bible. Settlement patterns are linked principally to climate and water sources. The Negev, the desert areas, and the Dead Sea—with their lack of precipitation—have mainly served as temporary settlement regions for seminomadic populations engaged in rudimentary forms of agriculture. The northern climatic belt has a completely different settlement character partly because of its milder weather and greater precipitation. Historically, the north contained more permanent sites and centers of agricultural activity. Throughout its history, this northern area has been more populous than the south.

The contrast between the desert and the cultivated land has resulted in much conflict between peoples dwelling in those differing regions. Desert marauders such as the Amalekites and Midianites proved to be a most dangerous opponent of Israel. The people of God, who lived primarily in the hill country and were mostly agriculturists, seemed always at odds with the frontier people. Saul, for instance, thought it so necessary to secure Israel's borders from desert invasion that he mounted a major military campaign against the desert tribes (1 Sam 14:47–48).

Climate has largely determined the economy of the land of the Bible. In ancient times, agriculture was the basis of Palestine's economy. Areas that receive sufficient precipitation have the capacity to sustain natural farming, and therefore have a significant agricultural advantage. Biblical Israel was inhabited mainly by a highland people residing in the Judean and Samaritan mountains. Because those regions receive substantial rainfall and have fertile soils, they can sustain considerable agricultural capacity. Both cereals and deciduous fruit grow in this region. These advantages led Israel to develop an economy based principally on agriculture.

Vegetation

Climate, topography, and soils are the primary factors in determining vegetation or plant geography. Climate provides favorable or unfavorable thermal and rainfall conditions, such as necessary water for plant growth; topography supplies a surface configuration suitable to specific plant associations; and soils provide nutrients necessary for particular plants. Within the land of the Bible, significant variations exist in each of these factors, as previously indicated. As a result, Palestine is a land of many floral contrasts.

Four districts of plant types or associations may be distinguished in the land of the Bible. These districts correspond to the four climatic zones discussed previously.

1. *Mediterranean (wet zone) flora.* This zone is the largest of the vegetation districts in the land of the Bible and receives on average about fourteen inches of precipitation per year. The plants in the Mediterranean zone are distributed over two widely divergent landscapes: the hilly regions and the coastal areas. The hill country was characterized in Bible times as a climatic district of evergreen maquis and forests. In these hills would be found extensive shrub vegetation with scattered full-sized trees such as evergreen oak, terebinth, and Jerusalem pine. Many of the trees have disappeared because of deforestation, but meager remnants of the evergreen maquis are preserved in areas such as Mount Carmel.

The valleys and coastal areas of Palestine have shorter plants than the highlands. These areas are typified by a dense carpet of low shrubs and a scattering of carob trees.

2. *Irano-Turonian (dry steppe) plant life.* Receiving a mere six to twelve inches of rain per year, this district can maintain only a sparse vegetation cover. Characteristic of this plant association are low brush or dwarf bushes. This form of plant life is centered principally in the Beersheba region.

3. *Arabian (desert) floral zone.* This district comprises the desert regions of Palestine, including the Dead Sea area, the Judean desert, most of the Negev, and most of the Sinai plateau. It contains desert vegetation in which plant cover is sporadic. Many areas are barren. The greatest concentration of vegetation appears in wadi beds where plants grow because of winter floods.

4. *Sudanese (oasis) vegetation.* This area includes over forty plant types that need both high temperatures and abundant water. The oasis spots in the land of the Bible (En Gedi, Jericho, etc.) provide just the kind of environment needed for this variety of plant life. As previously mentioned, the lotus tree is the most significant plant of this district.

Agriculture was the foundation of most economies of antiquity in the land of the Bible. Israel, which was located principally in the hilly regions of the Mediterranean climatic and floral zone, was an agrarian society. In contrast to peoples who lived in the Negev and Sinai, the Hebrews used little irrigation for farming because precipitation was sufficiently high for them to do natural farming. Scripture specifically describes Israel's blessing in this regard: "But the land into which you are about to cross to possess it, a land of hills and valleys, drinks water from the rain of heaven, a land for which the Lord your God cares" (Deut. 11:11–12 NASB).

The agricultural products grown by the Israelites in the hill country are also described in the Bible. They include horticultural products as well as cereals. "For the Lord your God is bringing you into a good land, a land of brooks of water, of fountains and springs, flowing forth in valleys and hills; a land of wheat and barley, of vines and fig trees and pomegranates, a land of olive oil and honey" (Deut. 8:7–8 NASB).

The Israelites worked a significant number of crops. At the Israelite site of Gezer, archaeologists discovered a clay tablet with Hebrew writing that described the basic agricultural year. It reads,

> *His two months are olive harvesting,*
> *His two months are planting grain,*
> *His two months are late planting,*
> *His month is hoeing flax,*
> *His month is barley harvest,*
> *His month is harvest and festivals,*
> *His two months are vine tending,*
> *His month is summer fruit.*

Although the substantial rainfall of the Judean and Samaritan mountains was an advantage to Israelite agriculture, the steep terrain was a problem. In their natural state, the severe slopes of most of the mountainous regions make cultivation virtually impossible. Water rushes down the mountainsides, eroding the soil. As a consequence, the soil cover of the highlands is extremely shallow. In addition, a particularly rocky soil characterizes the area. These factors made the highlands a difficult region for agriculture.

However, the Hebrews established favorable, continuous, and extensive agricultural conditions on the sloping areas by terracing the land. Terracing is a man-made system by which slopes of hills are transformed into a series of flat, horizontal surfaces. It has three functions: to prevent erosion, to increase the accumulation of water and soil, and to remove rocks from the soil by using them for terrace walls. In this way, the Israelites could utilize land that previously was of limited agricultural value. Both deciduous fruit crops and cereals thrived on these sloping areas.

To create more land for agriculture, the Israelites cleared trees in the highlands. The book of Joshua explains, "Then the sons of Joseph spoke to Joshua, saying, 'Why have you given me only one lot and one portion for an inheritance, since I am a numerous people whom the Lord has thus far blessed?' And Joshua said to them, 'If you are a numerous people, go up to the forest and clear a place for yourself there in the land. . . . the hill country shall be yours. For though it is a forest, you shall clear it' " (Joshua 17:14–18 NASB).

Another important innovation in agriculture was the introduction of the beam press used for manufacturing olive oil. Archaeological discoveries of oil presses at the Hebrew sites of Beth Shemesh, Dan, Gezer, and Tell Beit Mirsim demonstrate that they were in widespread use no later than the eighth century B.C.

Some Israelites inhabited desert zones that required irrigation. Archaeologists have uncovered evidence that Hebrew farmers created terrace dams for cultivation in the desert in order to have greater control over the limited water supply. The Hebrews were developing or borrowing diversified agricultural techniques in order to cultivate areas that up until then had been only sparsely settled.

CHAPTER SIX

TOWNS AND CITIES
IN THE DAYS
OF THE PATRIARCHS
(Approximately 2000–1500 B.C.)

Up to this point, consideration has been limited to the topography of the land as designed by the Creator. But now it is time to turn to the structures of the human inhabitants as they moved forward under the cultural mandate of Creation to subdue the earth to the glory of God. According to the testimony of Scripture, the earliest efforts of a fallen humanity to establish cities were not directed to God's glory. These early builders named their cities after themselves, showing that they had no sense of obligation to give honor to their Creator in their accomplishments (cf. Gen. 4:17; 11:4).

With the arrival of God's people in the land, this circumstance changed somewhat. Now certain places gave honor to the Lord by their designations, such as *Beth-el,* meaning "house of God." Other places, such as Shechem, while retaining the names given them by their original inhabitants, took on new significance as a consequence of God's work for his people at that locale. In any case, the Lord was advancing his purposes of redemption in this territory. In considering these places of prominence, a more helpful perspective may be gained by following the trail of historical progression throughout Scripture rather than retracing the outline of the various geographical sections previously indicated. Some cities and towns achieve prominence in one specific era of redemptive history, while others grow in significance across the centuries. It is in this context of historical progression that the importance of these cities may be understood most fully.

A number of cities played a prominent role in the lives of Abraham, Isaac, Jacob, and Joseph. Six cities deserve special notice: Shechem, Bethel, (Jeru)salem, Hebron, Beersheba, and Peniel (see Map 6).

Shechem

Abraham offered his initial sacrifice to the Lord in the Land of Promise at Shechem, for there the Lord indicated for the first time that this was the specified land that would belong to him and his descendants (Gen. 12:6–7). Before this time, Abraham had followed the normal trail of caravans moving from Ur of the Chaldees along the Tigris-Euphrates valley to Haran in Syria and then down into the land of the Canaanites. The Lord had commanded that the Patriarch leave his homeland and travel to a place that God would show him. Yet it was only when he reached Shechem in the course of his travels that the Lord identified the land that was to be his.

The city of Shechem is located at a major crossroads in central Palestine. Situated at the eastern end of the passageway

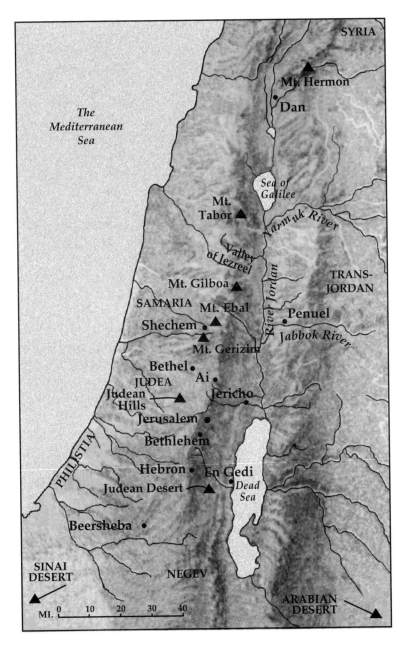

Map 6. Towns and Cities in the Days of the Patriarchs

between the mountains known as Gerizim and Ebal, this city has played host to numerous major roads that pass through the central hills.

It should not be supposed that this choice spot was virtually vacant, a ripe plum ready for Abraham's picking. Much to the contrary, "the Canaanites were in the land," as Scripture indicates (Gen. 12:6). The trial of Abraham's faith does not end with his arrival in the Land of Promise. He must now undergo a different kind of test. Earlier he had been required to wander without knowing the identity of the land the Lord would give him. Now he must live with the knowledge that this indeed is his Land of Promise, though it is possessed by someone else.

Rather fascinating extrabiblical evidence discovered in Egypt confirms the presence of other peoples in Shechem during this same time period. Pottery bowls and clay figurines now known as the "execration texts" bear inscribed curses against the enemies of Egypt. The pharaoh would smash these engraved objects as a means of placing a curse on his enemies. Apparently Shechem is mentioned as a defeated enemy of Egypt on one of these texts dating from the nineteenth century B.C. (Pfeiffer 1966, 518). In addition, the fourteenth-century-B.C. letters addressed to the Egyptian pharaoh at Amarna (located between Cairo and Luxor) refer to the inhabitants of Shechem as conspirators with the foreign Habiru in creating great disorder and civic unrest among the cities of Canaan. Clearly, from biblical as well as extrabiblical sources, Shechem was anything but a choice "vacant lot" in the days of the patriarchs.

After his fourteen-year absence from the Land of Promise, Jacob followed in the footsteps of his grandfather Abraham by making Shechem his first stop. There he took a dramatic step toward claiming for himself the promise concerning the land. He bought a parcel of ground from the sons of Hamor, the father of Shechem, as a place to pitch his tent. Except for the burial plot bought earlier by Abraham, the possession of the land would have its beginning at this place. Here Jacob, whose name had just recently been changed to Israel, built an altar dedicated to "God, the God of Israel" (Gen. 33:18–20).

But the possession of the promises would not flow easily from this point. Living so close to the Canaanites created problems. A Canaanite nobleman from Shechem violated Dinah the daughter of Jacob. In revenge, Simeon and Levi treacherously slaughtered all the men of Shechem. At that point, the family of Jacob was forced to move from the area because of the offense created among the inhabitants of the land (Gen. 34:1–31).

Some five hundred years later, the descendants of Jacob re-entered the Land of Promise. As soon as Joshua and his people cleared the way by defeating Jericho and Ai, they headed for Shechem. Precisely at the place that had been indicated by Moses, the nation read to themselves the curses and the blessings of the law as alternative outworkings of the covenant relationship established between themselves and the Lord (Deut. 11:29–30; Josh. 8:30–35).

Once more, at the end of the period of conquest, Joshua assembled the people at Shechem for a renewal of the covenant. He committed them to the Lord and rehearsed the Lord's commitment to them. After reading the whole of the law, he raised up a stone of testimony against them should they prove unfaithful to the covenant. Here also Joshua buried the bones of Joseph in the same piece of property that Jacob had bought from the sons of Hamor, the father of Shechem (Josh. 24:1–32).[1]

---

1. The site identified as Shechem has proved to be a valuable source of religious icons related to Canaanite cultic shrines dating to the period of the patriarchs. The archaeological record demonstrates that this city was an important center of pagan worship in Middle-Bronze Palestine (1900–1500 B.C.). Extensive excavations of the mound known as Tell Balatah have revealed a significant town surrounded by an elaborate fortification system with several gates dating from 1750 to 1650 B.C. Inside massive walls was an acropolis separated from the rest of the occupation. Several large and important "courtyard" temples were uncovered as well. It has been suggested that the covenant renewal under Joshua took place in the excavated Fortress Temple at Shechem. This structure originally was built in the seventeenth century B.C., and may have been the worship center designated as El-Berith in Judges 9:46.

At this place centuries later, the bones of the patriarch were resting in his tomb when the voice of One who was Jacob's descendant spoke significant words that would effect their future. At the well of Sychar (Shechem) this One promised the water of eternal life to a woman enslaved by sin (John 4:1–26). Through him the way was opened to the ultimate fulfillment of the promises of possession of the land that had been spoken so many centuries earlier to the patriarchs. The blessings of paradise promised to the fathers could become the possession of all sinners who would come to him for life.

Bethel

The locale of Bethel lies at a second major crossroads of north-south and east-west passages through central Palestine. Northward is Shechem and Samaria; southward is Jerusalem and Hebron. To the west, a major valley leads to the Mediterranean trade route; and to the east, a short journey brings the traveler to Jericho, the place of the major ford across the Jordan in the area. It is not surprising that Jeroboam, the first king of the northern empire, set up his rival altar at the Bethel crossroads (1 Kings 12:26–29). All the male pilgrims making their way to Jerusalem three times a year for their annual festivals would feel at first that they were making the familiar trek to the traditional site of worship. If they took the central route through Palestine, they would simply stop ten miles sooner. If they passed through Jericho, they would angle slightly northward and arrive at Bethel rather than Jerusalem.[2]

---

2. Excavations at modern Beitin, which possibly could be identified as the biblical Bethel, have revealed a flourishing Canaanite city in the patriarchal period of the Middle Bronze Age (1900–1500 B.C.). The city was strongly defended by a massive outer wall measuring 3.5 meters thick and four well-fortified gate complexes. A large Canaanite sanctuary has been uncovered just inside the city wall. This sacred site contained remains of a large quantity of cultic materials, including storage jars with serpent symbols, animal bones, and ritual ceramic ware.

Bethel had its own sacred traditions, traditions that determined its name. As Jacob made his way northward to avoid the ire of his brother Esau, he spent the night at the site of Bethel, which previously had been known as Luz. Shortly before leaving the Land of Promise for a fourteen-year absence, Jacob had a dream in which he saw a troop of angels ascending and descending a ladder that reached into God's presence (Gen. 28:10–22). How could he ever forget this place? For it was the gate of heaven, nothing less than *Beth-el,* the "house of God." When he finally returned to the Land of Promise, the Lord instructed Jacob to consecrate himself once more by building an altar at Bethel (Gen. 35:1–15).

In a later era, a descendent of this same Jacob experienced a higher privilege than his esteemed ancestor. Rather than appearing in the form of a dream, this new "ladder" that led into the presence of God stood before Nathanael in flesh and blood. This living Way to the presence of the Lord was embodied in the person of God's Son. On him the descendants of Jacob could expect to see the angels of God ascending and descending. Far better than the sacred place of Bethel would be this sacred Son of Man who himself provided immediate access into the presence of the Father (John 1:49–51).

(Jeru)salem[3]

As Abraham journeyed twelve miles farther south on the road that runs along the spine of the central ridge of mountains in Palestine, he would have come to the site of Salem. Better known as Jerusalem, this most important of all cities in the history of redemption is located at the northernmost point of the Judean hills. From the earliest period in Israelite history, Jerusalem had a vital role to play.[4]

---

3. For additional treatments of Jerusalem, see pp. 83, 94, 120.
4. The Jebusite or Canaanite city of Jerusalem was located on a hill known as "Ophel," located in the southeastern segment of the modern city. Its

First came Melchizedek, king of Jerusalem. In the book of Genesis, whose whole structure builds around ten different "genealogies," this mysterious figure appears on the stage of history as a genuine anomaly. Because Scripture provides no record of his line of descent, he appropriately is described as being "without father or mother" (Heb. 7:3). As a rare exception to the closely regulated pattern of the Old Testament, Melchizedek combines the offices of priest and king. He rules over the ancient city-state of (Jeru)salem, while also functioning as "priest of God Most High" (Gen. 14:18). To him great Abraham paid a tithe, and from him great Abraham received a blessing. Since it is self-evident that the lesser is blessed by the greater, Melchizedek of Jerusalem must be, in the redemptive purposes of God, greater than Abraham (Heb. 7:7). This conclusion is confirmed ultimately by the fact that the priesthood of the Lord Jesus Christ is reckoned to be of the eternal order foreshadowed by the man Melchizedek rather than of the temporal order of Levi, the descendant of Abraham (Heb. 7:14–16).

In addition to presenting a tithe to Jerusalem's king, Abraham subsequently offered another sacrifice in the locale of this king's domain. On Mount Moriah at Jerusalem, Abraham bound to the altar his only son, the son whom he loved (Gen. 22:9–10). Happily the Patriarch is required to execute this sacrifice only in his heart, since the Lord stays the knife and himself supplies a substitute ram for the altar. But this place must be perpetually memorialized. For here in the locale of Mount Moriah at Jerusalem David offers his atoning sacrifice to stay the consuming wrath of God (1 Chron. 21:25–26); here Solomon builds his glorious temple so that perpetual sacrifices may be offered to the Lord across the

---

habitation dates back into the Chalcolithic period (third millennium B.C.). Recent excavations have uncovered a city wall dating to Middle Bronze II (1900–1500 B.C.), the time of the patriarchs. Jerusalem's ancient significance is indicated further by its mention in Egyptian texts as early as the twentieth century B.C.

centuries (2 Chron. 3:1); and here eventually the Lamb of God that takes away the sin of the world offers the body that God has prepared for him as a sacrifice to be offered once for sin (Heb. 10:5).

Hebron[5]

As Abraham followed the patriarchal highway southward for an additional twenty miles below Jerusalem, he would come to the town of Hebron. Otherwise known as Mamre, Hebron is situated on the highest peak of Palestine proper. From this vantage point, the Patriarch could see the fault of the Dead Sea across the barren Judean desert to the east, and could look westward onto fertile Philistine territory along the shores of the Mediterranean. A challenging but often-traveled trail leads downward from the peaks of Hebron at over three thousand feet above sea level to the springs of En Gedi far below on the shore of the Dead Sea. At 1,300 feet below sea level, this is the earth's lowest depression. In a span of approximately twenty miles, the drop is over 4,500 feet.

The drastic difference between these two regions, high Hebron and the fertile valley around the Jordan, became a major point of dissension between Abraham and his nephew Lot. Though promised by God the whole of the land, Abraham generously offered his youthful, eager relative first choice of all the land (Gen. 13:8–9). Moved by something less than the best of motives, Lot chose for himself the fertile plains of the Jordan (Gen. 13:10–11). But after Lot had parted from him, the Lord himself appeared to Abraham and reassured him that ultimately the whole land would belong to him and his seed (Gen. 13:14–17).

With this promise fresh in his mind, Abraham settled at Hebron with the vistas available from this high peak as a constant reminder of the Lord's expansive promise. Appropriately,

5. For further treatment of Hebron, see p. 93.

here Abraham also built an altar to the Lord (Gen. 13:18).

After many years of wandering as a nomad, Abraham returned to Hebron near the end of his life. Here his faithful companion Sarah died. At this sad moment, the Patriarch finally comes into possession of one small portion of the land that had been promised him. He bargains with a Hittite landowner for a plot of ground with a cave for the burial of Sarah (Gen. 23:17–20). Eventually Abraham himself, along with Isaac, Rebekah, and Leah would be buried here. Years afterward, weeping Joseph would return to this place accompanied by his royal Egyptian entourage to bury the embalmed body of his father Jacob (Gen. 50:12–13). In faithfulness to his word, Joseph honored the insistent demand of his father that he be buried in the Promised Land of Canaan rather than in Egypt (Gen. 50:4–5).

But what difference could it make to Jacob after he was dead? And why should the sons of Israel, despite all their haste, carry with them the bones of Joseph as they left Egypt four hundred years later? Was it purely for sentimental reasons that the patriarchs insisted on burial in this land, the Land of Promise? The testimony of Scripture suggests that the trial of their faith served as a school in which the Lord taught them to expect something beyond this life. Abraham, it is said, "was looking forward to the city with foundations, whose architect and builder is God" (Heb. 11:10). The voice from the bush that spoke to Moses long after the last patriarch had died declared, "I *am*" the God of Abraham, Isaac, and Jacob (Ex. 3:6), not "I *was*" their God. If he is the God of the living and not the dead, then Abraham, Isaac, and Jacob still must be around, waiting for the fulfillment of the promises of God that they never experienced in this life (Matt. 22:31–32).

So burial at Hebron, the premier peak for viewing the Land of Promise, suggests the hope of the patriarchs for resurrection from the dead. One day they will awaken from their tombs and look with new eyes on the land the Lord has given them, a land that has expanded under the new covenant to include the whole of the cosmos (Rom. 4:13). The fulfillment of the promises of the covenant-keeping God will be beyond their wildest imaginations.

When Israel got to the borders of the Land of Promise after their four-hundred-year sojourn in Egypt, the twelve appointed spies came to Hebron, where they heard of the giants among men that lived in the area (Num. 13:21–22). They delighted in sampling the grape cluster brought back to the camp as proof of the fruitfulness of the land. But their doubts overcame them, and because of their unbelief they were sentenced to forty years of wandering in the wilderness. Not yet would they enjoy the fruit of fertile Hebron.

Later, under Joshua's leadership, Hebron was conquered by the Israelite army when Hebron's king made the mistake of joining the southern coalition of Canaanite kings (Josh. 10:1–27). Ultimately, Caleb of Judah claimed the town in accord with the promise made to him by Moses because of his full-of-faith report as one of the original twelve that spied out the land (Josh. 14:6–15).

Beersheba

In following the natural trail that Abraham and the other patriarchs would have taken as they journeyed in a southerly direction through the central section of the land, the traveler would come first to Shechem as the central point of Samaria in the north. Then after passing through Bethel and Jerusalem, he would arrive at Hebron as the heart of Judah to the south. Finally he would descend to Beersheba, situated at the center of the Negev on the road leading to Egypt. An international traveler who had no business in Palestine proper would have taken "the way of the sea" along the Mediterranean coastline, or possibly the King's Highway along the high flatlands in Transjordan that skirt the eastern edge of the Arabian desert. But the person who had his business in this land would have followed exactly the path traveled by the biblical patriarchs, with his journey leading him through these places and eventually to Beersheba.

Beersheba sits on the northern edge of the Sinai desert along the fluctuating line of grazable territory that ebbs and flows into the barrenness of Sinai depending on how far south the rain falls from one year to the next. The town itself remains stable only because it does not depend on rain for its water supply.

Two biblical narratives surround the naming of this town, one associated with Abraham and one with his son Isaac. In both cases, Abimelech, a king in the coastal region of Philistia, seeks the good will of the biblical patriarchs. The Philistine ruler is settled and secure in his own land, but he observes that God's greater blessing rests on these landless wanderers. Even though Abraham has a complaint against Abimelech's servants for seizing one of the wells he has dug, he is the one who brings forward seven lambs as a sacrifice to seal a covenant of peace between himself and Abimelech. As a result of this action, the place is called *Beersheba,* meaning either "well of the oath" or "well of seven." Even in modern times it has been attested that seven wells distinguish the locale of this city (Smith 1972, 193f.). Once the Philistine monarch has departed, Abraham plants a tamarisk tree in Beersheba, indicating that he senses himself to be one step closer to the actual possession of the promises (Gen. 21:22–32).

The similarities between this interchange between Abraham and Abimelech and the subsequent incident involving Isaac have led some people to conclude that different authors must have reported the same incident, though exchanging Isaac for Abraham. But the overall pattern of Isaac's life creates the expectation of exactly this kind of repetition. Isaac's character has a passive element that climaxes with his submission even to the point of allowing himself to be bound to the altar of sacrifice by his aging father. So it is not surprising that he spends a great deal of time digging again the same wells that had been dug by his father. In a similar way, he confirms a similar oath with Abimelech at Beersheba. As he had renamed the wells that he redug with exactly the same names as those originally given them by his father Abraham (Gen. 26:18), so he also reconfirms the significance of this place called "Beersheba" when his men bring the report that they had struck water exactly on the day that the treaty of peace was sealed with Abimelech (Gen. 26:32).

Through subsequent centuries, this outpost claimed by Abraham and his descendants has served as the southernmost measure of the land. The scope of the Promised Land always has been reckoned from varied starting points north, but always ". . . to Beersheba" in the south. So the kingdom originally was measured "from Dan to Beersheba" (Judg. 20:1; 1 Sam. 3:20; 2 Sam. 3:10; 17:11; 24:15; 1 Kings 4:25; 2 Chron. 30:5). After the schism the abbreviated measure was taken "from Geba to Beersheba" (2 Kings 23:8). Subsequent to the return from exile, it was "from Beersheba to the Valley of Hinnom" (Neh. 11:27, 30). With all the variations across the centuries, Beersheba has remained stable as the anchor-point of the kingdom's southern border.

But what if some day in the future the rains in Palestine should shift radically southward? What are the implications of the prophecies that declare that the desert shall blossom and bloom (Isa. 35:1)? Where then will the borders of the Promised Land set their new anchor? Is it conceivable that Beersheba will be replaced by another border city that seals a more lasting peace among men?

Perhaps the prophetic declarations about the transformation of the desert intend to indicate that the ancient borders of the Land of Promise are not large enough to embrace their anticipations of the future. Perhaps God has intended all along to expand this limited, tightly bordered realm of his blessing far beyond anything the patriarchs might have imagined. For did not the Lord indicate from the beginning that in the one man Abraham all the nations of the world would be blessed? And is not the expectation of God's people ultimately directed toward a new heavens and a new earth, when the shadowy old covenant image of return to the land is replaced by entrance into a restored paradise?

Peniel

Last of the towns to be noted because of their significance in the days of the patriarchs is Peniel. Located on the banks of the Jabbok in Transjordan, this place is situated outside the normal path followed by the patriarchs. But this was the place that the Angel of the Lord chose to confront Jacob as he returned to Palestine with his family after fleeing from Esau fourteen years earlier. The Lord wrestled with this devious man until the break of day, and in turn this man whose name (Jacob) means "supplanter" wrestled with God until he received a blessing. As a consequence, the patriarch had his name changed from "Jacob" to "Israel," the one who is "prince with God." This place was named *Peniel,* for Jacob had seen the "face of God" (Gen. 32:29–30).

But the people of Peniel had trouble living up to the honor associated with God's appearing to their forefather in this place. Some five hundred years later, Gideon and his courageous three hundred pursued the fifteen-thousand-strong remnant of the Midianite army. When they came to the town of Peniel, they were "faint, yet pursuing" (Judg. 8:4 KJV). All they asked was enough bread to renew their strength so they could continue the devastation of the Lord's enemies. But the people of Peniel were playing politics. They had the bread; they saw the need. It was their fellow Israelites who were asking help. But the men of Peniel had their doubts about this small army of Gideon. They could only picture their Midianite oppressors returning to torment them if they aided the pursuing troop of Israel. So they refused to help.

Gideon warned them of the consequences of their cowardice. The precious tower of Peniel, perhaps a memorial to the Lord's appearance to Jacob, would be razed. Nothing sacred or secular would protect them from the righteous judgments of the Lord.

After completing his routing of the Midianite army, Gideon returned to the town of Peniel. He did exactly as he had said. He tore down the tower and put the leaders of the city to death. Though revered in the history of Israel, the place of Peniel could not exempt its inhabitants from their continuing responsibility to remain faithful in serving the Lord.

CHAPTER SEVEN

TOWNS AND CITIES DURING THE CONQUEST AND THE PERIOD OF THE JUDGES
(Approximately 1500–1000 B.C.)

The chronology of Israel's history during the conquest and the period of the judges has been seriously debated among scholars for a number of years. Though a case may be made for other options, the biblical evidence seems to support two conclusions that offer significant assistance in resolving dating problems of the period. First, the chronological note of 1 Kings 6:1 supports a fifteenth-century B.C. date for the Exodus and a fourteenth-century B.C. date for the conquest of the land. Second, the reference in Judges 10:6–7 to the combined oppression of the Ammonites and the Philistines as subsequently developed in the narrative of the book of Judges strongly suggests simultaneous judgeships in Israel. These two conclusions provide a framework for resolving most of the problems associated with the chronology of the period of the judges. Subsequent discussion will develop these two conclusions more fully.

Focal Cities of the Conquest

Three locations deserve special notice as places of particular significance during the period of Israel's conquest of the land: Jericho, Jerusalem, and Hazor. These three cities played a central role in the three major phases of Joshua's campaigns (see Map 7).

Jericho[1]

Recognized as the world's oldest known city, Jericho has a history that traces back as far as 8000 B.C. The stones at Jericho testify to the existence of a walled city of seven to eight acres by 7000 B.C. Situated eight hundred feet below sea level on the western edge of the Jordan valley, the heavily fortified city guarded the major entrance to central Palestine from the east. Called the "city of palms," it was located in a green valley that stood in starkest contrast to the dry Judean desert that extended along the difficult ascent to Jerusalem to the west.

Because of its strategic location, Jericho could not be ignored by peoples entering Palestine from the east. Either the fortress must be conquered, or the invaders must expect endless harassment by excursionary forces issuing from its walls day and night. Joshua and the Israelites somehow had to nullify the threat implicit in the imposing battlements of Jericho as they entered the land.

---

1. For further treatment of Jericho, see p. 119.

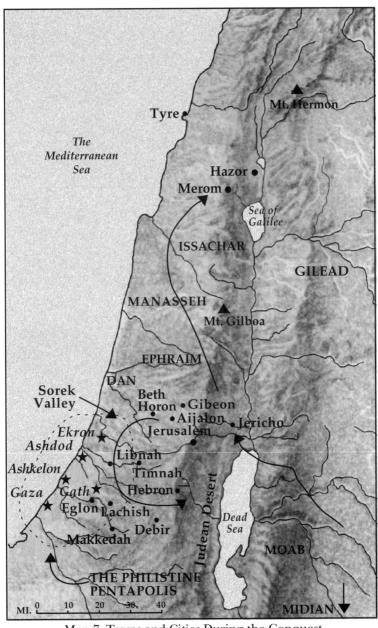

Map 7. Towns and Cities During the Conquest
and the Period of the Judges

God's way of dealing with Jericho was not man's way. So it is not surprising that modern scholarship has relegated the biblical account to the realm of dramatized fiction. One respected author has stated, "The biblical tradition speaks only in legendary terms about the conquest of Jericho . . ." (Aharoni 1967, 192). But the biblical account is offered in a straightforward narrative form which describes a process of conquest that corresponds to the sabbatical principle regarding restoration of lost land. After six days of marching around the city, the troops of Israel make the trek seven times on the seventh day. Then in response to the blast from the trumpets by the priests, the Lord gives them the land that had been denied them over the previous four hundred years (Josh. 6:1–21; cf. Lev. 25:8–13). This gracious gift of land was granted to God's people in a manner appropriate to the sabbatical principles inherent in God's governance of the world since Creation.

Earlier archaeological evidence had been read in a way that confirmed the biblical testimony concerning the dating of Israel's conquest. Scarabs discovered at Jericho were dated to the time of Amenhotep III of Egypt, who reigned alone until about 1385 B.C. when his son—the heretical Akhenaton—became co-regent. In the absence at Jericho of scarabs or pottery of this new era, a date for the destruction of the city was set that conformed to the biblical chronology of 1 Kings 6:1 (Garstang 1948, 135; cf. Pfeiffer 1966, 308). Later investigations of the ruins of Jericho, however, have interpreted the evidence in a more ambiguous manner. Yet even these interpretations have dated the latest occupancy of Jericho in this era "to the third quarter of the fourteenth century B.C.," which would fall between 1350 and 1325 B.C., only twenty to fifty years later than the most likely biblical chronology (cf. Kenyon 1957, 262). In any case, this later interpretation of the materials uncovered at Jericho offers no support to the critic's favored dating of the Exodus in the thirteenth century B.C. A more recent discussion of the data has pointed to a date of about 1430 B.C. for the fall of Jericho (see Bimson 1978, 144). In the end, the biblical record of the conquest of Jericho continues to commend itself as a trustworthy account of the entrance of God's people into the Land of Promise, and its brief chronological notes stand as testimony to the historical reality of these events.[2]

Jerusalem[3]

Hardly a period exists in biblical history when Jerusalem does not play a prominent role. The period of conquest is no exception, although the city destined to be God's chosen place on earth now comes to the fore because it provided a leader among God's enemies. The king of this prominent city-state in Joshua's day is identified as Adoni-Zedek. His name means "My Lord is righteousness," which is virtually identical in meaning with Melchizedek, the name of the king of Jerusalem in Abraham's day. Could it be that these two kings of the same city having essentially the same name are somehow related to one another? Could a single dynasty have ruled over Jerusalem across the five hundred years separating Abraham from Joshua? It is difficult to determine the answer to this question. But clearly the upright character found in Melchizedek is not reflected in the person of Adoni-Zedek. When the leaders of the neighboring town of Gibeon voluntarily surrender to Israel, Adoni-Zedek takes the initiative in summoning several prominent Canaanite kings of southern Palestine to join him in a coalition that will punish the Gibeonites as a way of intimidating any other towns that might consider capitulation to Joshua and his troops (Josh. 10:1–5).

This action of the king of Jerusalem precipitated one of

---

2. This date for the fall of Jericho is supported in the article by Bryant Wood, "Did the Israelites conquer Jericho?," *Biblical Archaeology Review* 16:2 (1990):44–58. Based on a reevaluation of the original excavation reports analyzing pottery, stratigraphy, scarab data, and carbon 14 testing, Wood concludes that Jericho was destroyed at the end of the Late Bronze I period, about 1400 B.C.

3. For additional treatments of Jerusalem, see pp. 69, 94. 120

the most dramatic moments in the history of the Bible. Joshua and his men march all night from Jericho to intercept the coalition of the five kings marching against Gibeon, their newest ally. They pursue the assembled enemy along the ascent to Beth Horon, ten miles northwest of Jerusalem. As they begin the descent into the valley of Aijalon, Joshua sees that daylight hours will expire before he has brought his campaign to completion. So he asks the Lord to make the sun stand still, giving him an extension of time to pursue his enemies. On this day, the Lord hearkened to the voice of a man as never before and as never since. Having temporarily entombed the five kings of Canaan in a cave, he later returns with his troops and executes them as an example of how the Lord will subdue all the enemies of God's people. Then Joshua proceeds with a thoroughgoing rout of the Canaanite cities of the south, following a hooked arch through Makkedah, Libnah, Lachish, Eglon, Hebron, and Debir. The conflict instigated by the king of Jerusalem had so weakened the military resources of these cities that they offered little resistance to the assaults of Joshua's men. So in the end, the coalition of the Lord's enemies only served to advance the Lord's purposes in giving the land to his people (Josh. 10:6–43).

Hazor

The king of Hazor in the north served the purposes of the Lord in a way similar to the king of Jerusalem in the south. Having heard of the conquest of Jerusalem along with its allies, Jabin, king of Hazor, assembled a vast hoard at the waters of Merom to fight against Israel. But Joshua was not one to be intimidated by superior forces. He had seen the Lord fight for him, and he was prepared to move aggressively against this new coalition of forces. The Lord appeared to him and told him that he would be victorious over this new enemy as well. So Joshua's whole army came against their adversaries suddenly and defeated this entire assembled mass (Josh. 11:1–20).

Hazor as identified by archaeologists is located on one of the most massive mounds found anywhere in Palestine. Situated ten to fifteen miles north of the Sea of Galilee, this mound reaches a height of some 130 feet, indicating just how many civilizations must have risen and fallen on the site. It covers an area of some twenty-five acres, while the lower part of the city consisted of an additional 175 acres (cf. Pfeiffer 1966, 284; Aharoni 1967, 206). The peak population of Hazor has been estimated at about forty thousand, a very large community for the era. Scripture indicates that Joshua burned only Hazor among the cities of the north (Josh. 11:11, 13), which would have been appropriate since their king was the one who instituted the coalition of forces against Israel. By the period of the Judges, however, the city apparently was reestablished, as seen by their enslavement of Israel in the days of Deborah (Judg. 4:2). The army of this second "Jabin king of Canaan, who reigned in Hazor" was routed by Israel, and eventually the king himself was destroyed (Judg. 4:23–24).

Joshua battled to claim the whole of the land for approximately seven years. But these three principal campaigns against the flagship cities of Canaan embody the major thrusts of the conquest. At the end of his life it could be said that Joshua had taken the entire land, even though many pockets of Canaanite resistance remained (cf. Josh. 11:23).

The Domain of Israel's Judges

The judges who ruled Israel from Joshua to Saul originated from a number of different locales in the land. Most of them clearly were regional in their responsibilities. Among the more prominent were:

- Othniel of Judah, son-in-law of Caleb, who took the town of Debir in the south (Judg. 1:13)
- Ehud of Benjamin, who delivered Israel from Eglon

of Moab (Judg. 3:15, 30)

- Gideon of Manasseh, who delivered Israel from Midian (Judg. 6:14–15)
- Tola of Issachar, who made his home in the hill country of Ephraim (Judg. 10:1–2)

Noteworthy is the record of two judges who apparently operated simultaneously but independently of one another in different sections of the country: Jephthah of Gilead and Samson of Dan. The book of Judges sets the stage for their work by indicating that because of Israel's sin the Lord "sold them into the hands of the Philistines and the Ammonites" (Judg. 10:7). Then the narrative proceeds to recount the deliverance of Israel, first from the Ammonites by Jephthah in Gilead (Judg. 11–12), and then from the Philistines by Samson along the plains of the Mediterranean (Judg. 13–16). Since Gilead is located to the northeast in Transjordan while Philistia is located to the southwest on the way to Egypt, it is quite reasonable to presume that these judgeships occurred simultaneously. Yet certain distinctives may be indicated about these two areas and the deliverances accomplished by their respective judges.

Gilead

Gilead has been known across the centuries for its beautiful pasturelands, its legendary balm, and the security it provided for any number of people fleeing from their adversaries. Joseph was sold to a caravan of Ishmaelites coming down from Gilead, whose camels "were loaded with spices, balm and myrrh" (Gen. 37:25). The "balm of Gilead" also is mentioned in other passages of Scripture (cf. Jer. 8:22; 46:11; Ezek 27:17). This high plateau in Transjordan served as a place of refuge for the family of Saul after the tragic events at Mount Gilboa, for David when he fled from his son Absalom, and for the survivors of the destruction of Jerusalem in the first century A.D. (2 Sam. 2:8; 17:21–22; cf. Baly 1957, 228, 229). The people of Jabesh in Gilead displayed the fierce loyalty they had developed for Saul when he delivered them from the threat of the Ammonites by crossing the Jordan and taking the body of Saul from the walls of Beth Shan so that the slain king might have a decent burial (1 Sam. 31:11–13).

The Philistine Pentapolis

Five noteworthy Philistine cities were located in the coastal plain of southern Palestine: Gaza, Gath, Ashkelon, Ashdod, and Ekron. They are frequently referred to as the "Philistine pentapolis." Part of the original inheritance of the tribe of Dan lay in this area, which meant that this small tribe had little peace. Living so close to their archenemies meant that this tribe constantly faced pressures to compromise. So it is not surprising to find Samson of the tribe of Dan wandering a few hundred yards down the Sorek valley to Timnah where he found a Philistine girl he wanted to marry. At first his mother loudly protested, but finally she consented to their union. But some months after the wedding, when Samson returned to claim his bride, he discovered that she had been given by the Philistines to someone else. Eventually the struggle between Samson and his Philistine neighbors led to his own death along with a large number of the Philistine nobility (Judg. 14–16).

Virtually all the various sections of the Land of Promise had their "judge"—their deliverer—at one time or another. The Lord was gracious in not ignoring the needs of any of his people, even though their own sin was primarily the cause of their calamity.

CHAPTER EIGHT

TOWNS AND CITIES
DURING THE
UNITED AND DIVIDED
MONARCHIES
(Approximately 1000–500 B.C.)

The period of the judges is characterized as an era of chaos because "in those days there was no king in Israel, but every man did that which was right in his own eyes" (Judg. 17:6 KJV; see also 18:1; 19:1; 21:25). This epoch in Israel's history underscored the need of the nation for a king, even though in principle God himself was their ruler.

As Israel entered its era of kingship, certain cities came into prominence. Most significant were Gibeah, Hebron,

Jerusalem, Samaria, Jezreel, Megiddo, and Lachish (see Map 8). In each case, the geographical situation of these cities had a major effect on the role they played in Israel's monarchy. Some of these places are associated with encouraging periods of advancement for God's kingdom on earth. Others recall sad moments of decline in the Lord's reign of righteousness. Together, the experiences of Israel under the monarchy point to the need for one greater than David or any of his descendants. The king chosen of the Lord must be taken from among his brothers so that he will be perceived as accessible to them all. But he also will need attributes of divine perfection and power essential for advancing a kingdom of grace in the midst of a fallen and perpetually sinful race.

Gibeah[1]

Located a short distance north of Jerusalem, the town of Gibeah was in Benjaminite territory. The record of its jaded history begins in the days of the judges, when a wandering Levite travels homeward after having fetched his straying concubine. The Levite's servant urges him to stay in Jerusalem in view of the descending darkness. But the man insists on pressing on to Gibeah since it was occupied by fellow Israelites, while Jerusalem at this time was in the hands of the heathen Canaanites. Contrary to the laws of hospitality in Israel requiring the housing of a stranger, no one in the city of Gibeah extends to the wandering brother an invitation to spend the

---

1. The first Iron Age town of Gibeah was founded in the twelfth century B.C. Archaeologists have uncovered a massive destruction of this city that dates to about 1100 B.C. The devastation of Gibeah by the Israelites as described in Judges 19–20 possibly could be evidenced by these remains. The city seems to have been rebuilt shortly after this destruction, featuring a rectangular fortress with thick walls and large corner towers. The ceramic work that has been uncovered dates the complex to the time of Saul. Another enormous ash layer at the same site may be identified with the conquest of Nebuchadnezzar in 587–86 B.C.

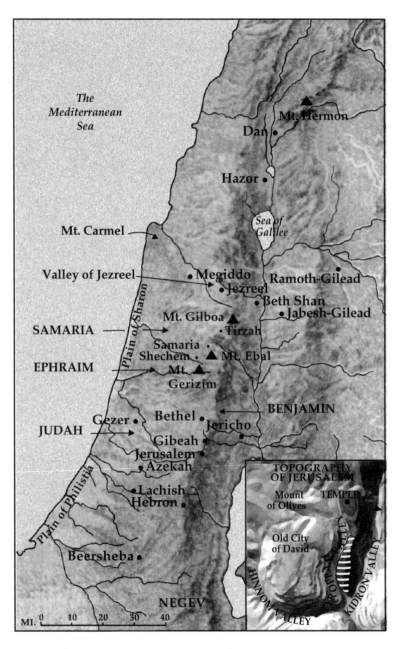

Map 8. Towns and Cities During the United and Divided Monarchies

91

night. An old man who himself is a sojourner fulfills the duty. But during the night, the men of this Benjaminite city demand that the old man make his guest available to them so they can "know" him, referring to acts of a sexually perverted nature. In response, the two men inside offer the Levite's concubine, who is so abused during the night that she lies dead at their doorstep the next morning. In an effort to deal with this abominable situation, all the tribes of Israel assemble to execute justice on the inhabitants of the city. But the Benjaminite tribe determines to intervene in defense of their brothers from Gibeah.

In several successive battles, numerous Israelites from the various tribes perish. Only six hundred males from the entire tribe of Benjamin survive. The nation is repulsed by the thought of having a tribe of Israel eliminated from their ranks. Since a number of women have survived the punishment brought on Jabesh Gilead for their refusal to support the military action against Gibeah, these women are given as wives to the remaining Benjaminites. But still, a few of the surviving Benjaminites have no mates. So the men of Israel "look the other way" while the remaining bachelors in Benjamin snatch brides for themselves from the other tribes of Israel at a particular religious festival. Appropriately, the writer of the book of Judges concludes this tale of human madness by indicating that in those days there was no king in Israel, and that as a consequence every man did that which was right in his own eyes (Judg. 19:1–21:25).

How evident is the grace of God when some years later the first king of Israel should come from the tribe of Benjamin and the town of Gibeah. After being anointed by Samuel as Israel's first monarch, Saul returned to his hometown of Gibeah to rule over the tribes of Israel. His first act of heroism was to rescue the inhabitants of Jabesh Gilead from the brutal threats of their Ammonite neighbors in Transjordan (1 Sam. 11:1–11).

It also is worth noting that the greatest Christian missionary ever to live descended from this spared remnant of the tribe of Benjamin. Paul, the Apostle to the Gentiles, identifies himself as a Hebrew of the Hebrews, a descendant of the tribe of Benjamin (Phil. 3:5). The chaos created by the worst of human actions eventually became subservient to God's most elevated purposes of grace.

Today the mound of ancient Gibeah stands just north of the city of Jerusalem. On its crest is the bare frame of a modern structure that never was completed. The king of the modern nation of Jordan once began to build a palace on the peak of Gibeah. But war interrupted his plans, and the project has never been completed.

Hebron[2]

Since Hebron was the only place in the Land of Promise where Abraham possessed some property, it is not surprising that David ended up settling in Hebron as the first capitol for his monarchy. Lying in the territory of Judah along the patriarchal highway, Hebron had the natural advantage of a thousand years of national honor. Here Abraham had buried Sarah, and here Isaac and Esau had returned to bury their father Abraham.

When Saul and his son Jonathan lost their lives in a battle with the Philistines at Mount Gilboa, David had to be extremely careful about every move he made. He asked the Lord if he should abandon his abode in the Negev and relocate in one of the cities of Judah. The Lord directed him to Hebron, where David settled with his family and his loyal followers (2 Sam. 2:1–3). Now the time had come for David to be recognized as king over Israel. But initially only David's own tribe, the tribe of Judah, would give him his rightful acknowledgment as the anointed of the Lord. So for seven and one-half years, David ruled Judah from Hebron, struggling throughout this period

---

2. For further background to Hebron, see p. 71.

with a divided nation (2 Sam. 2:4; 5:5). From Hebron he waged his war against Abner who supported Ish-Bosheth, son of Saul, in his claim on the crown. So Hebron continued to play a prominent role in the early days of the monarchy in Israel until the whole of the nation was ready to acknowledge David as the Lord's chosen and anointed king.

Sad to say, this town later became the staging ground for Absalom, David's ambitious and rebellious son. Absalom had been born in Hebron, and so it became a natural place for him to assert his rival leadership. Having wooed the hearts of the people away from David over a four-year period, the young aspirant secretly sent messengers to his compatriots throughout the land to meet him in Hebron. There he had himself declared king in place of David, and from there he launched his march to the capitulating capitol city of Jerusalem (2 Sam. 15:1–12).

From this point on, Hebron played only a minor role in the history of the nation. It is nowhere mentioned in the New Testament as a place of ministry for Christ or his disciples. It is as though the shame of being associated with Absalom's rebellion forced the eclipse of the once-prominent city. In any case, the prominence enjoyed by Hebron for a short while as the capitol of the nation was assumed by Jerusalem its successor. As John the Baptist fulfilled the role of forerunner to Jesus Christ, so Hebron preceded Jerusalem as the capitol city of the country.

Jerusalem[3]

Travel the land of God's appointment from Dan to Beersheba, and no place can be found quite like Jerusalem. Other locales might have presented themselves as more logical choices for the capitol of a united kingdom. Shechem, Shiloh, or Gibeah could offer the advantages of ancient honor as well as strategic positioning. But David chose Jerusalem, a city not even claimed

---

3. For additional treatments of Jerusalem, see pp. 63, 83, 120.

as Israelite territory in his own day. Though seized by Israel from the Canaanites in the days of the judges (Judg. 1:8), this site continued to fall back into the possession of the enemy. Four hundred years after the conquest and division of the land under Joshua, Jerusalem still remained under the control of the Jebusites. David would have to find good reasons to make this city his own.

And good reasons there were. Even the fact that the city was not under Israel's control could be regarded as a positive reason for David's designating it as his future capitol. For as time confirmed, this place would come to be known across the millennia as "the City of David." If it had not been taken by him, it might not have taken his name.

Jerusalem's geographical situation also supported its choice as a uniting capitol city. Surprise may arise from the traveler's first sight of the city, for the location of David's original town obviously is not by any means elevated above its neighboring ridges. As a matter of fact, the site is completely surrounded by higher hills. David's hill might be depicted as a single slice of pie remaining in a rounded pie pan.

Yet this seemingly lowly condition only serves to accentuate the prominence of the place. As a horseshoe-shaped amphitheater trains every eye to look down on the drama being enacted below, so the mountains surrounding Jerusalem afford a unique opportunity for men to gaze on its glory. It possesses a geological structure that is uniquely its own.

The V-shaped valleys that define the ridge called the city of David are formed by steep inclines. With a sturdy defensive wall situated at the top of these ascents, the city was virtually impregnable from three sides. Only toward the north was Jerusalem subject to serious threat from assaulting armies. It is quite understandable that David would offer special recognition to the man who took this city on his behalf (1 Chron. 11:6). There is a possibility that Joab succeeded in taking the town from the Jebusites only by entering through a water shaft that brought him inside the city's walls, not by storming its defenses (2 Sam. 5:8). The Jebusites, who claimed that the "lame and the blind" were quite adequate for Jerusalem's defense, had substantial ground for their boast (2 Sam. 5:6).[4]

This situation of the city provided an appropriate circumstance for Jerusalem's serving as earthly representation of the eternal city of God. Let all the nations gather about its perimeter and behold the beauty of the place where the God of heaven and earth reigns, for Jerusalem is "beautiful for situation" (Ps. 48:2–3 KJV). Let men see with their own eyes the security in which God's city dwells, for as long as the Lord is there, this place is invulnerable (Ps. 46:4–5). Let men from all nations witness the secured peace that abides here and come within its walls where they can find peace for themselves.

The political circumstance of Jerusalem offered a further reason for its choice by David. Most recently, the body politic of Israel had been rent by the struggle between Saul of Benjamin and David of Judah. Behind this contest was the ancient distinction between the two lines of descendency from the two wives of the patriarch Jacob. For Judah was of Leah and Benjamin of Rachel. Jacob's own prophetic utterance concerning the tribes that would descend from his sons set the stage for tension regarding the position of leadership within the nation. The scepter of rule would not depart from Judah, son of Leah (Gen. 49:10); but Joseph of Rachel, full brother to Benjamin, would have the preeminence (Gen. 49:26; Deut. 33:16). Immediately north of Benjamin was the larger territory of Ephraim, son of Joseph, who also descended from Rachel. Ephraim had held the prophesied station of dignity promised to Joseph through all the centuries since the

---

4. Remains of a vertical shaft and connecting tunnels that allowed Jerusalemites from inside the city to reach the Gihon Spring outside the city were found by early archaeologists. The vertical shaft, called "Warren's Shaft" after its discoverer, would have proven quite difficult to scale by enemies attempting to invade the city. Yet it may have been through these tunnels and up this shaft that Joab, along with David's men, penetrated the Jebusite city.

ark of the covenant, representing the throne of God on earth, had been located at Shiloh (Josh. 18:1, 8; 19:51; 21:2; Judg. 18:31; 21:19; 1 Sam. 1:3; 3:21; 4:3–4). Then the tribe of Benjamin, descended from Rachel, had stepped into the limelight of leadership with the designation of Saul the Benjaminite as the first king of Israel.

It was in this centuries-old context of political prominence for the tribes coming from Rachel that David of Judah became king over all Israel (2 Sam. 5:1–2). The northern coalition supporting Saul's son Ish-Bosheth finally had collapsed. Elders representing all the tribes of Israel came deep into the tribal territory of Judah to anoint David as king at Hebron. But it must have been immediately obvious to a man as astute as David that he could not reign effectively from this locale. But where could he go? Shechem was far too distant from his core of support in Judah. Shiloh of Ephraim would not suit him, for it was at that place that the dread word *Ichabod*, meaning "the Glory has departed," had been solemnly pronounced at the time of the Philistine capture of the ark (1 Sam. 4:21–22; cf. Ps. 78:60–61, 67–68; Jer. 7:12; 26:5–6, 9). Neither could Gibeah of Saul be regarded as a reasonable location for the capitol city of this man who had been pursued relentlessly by Saul for years.

But then there was this city of the Jebusites. And where was it? On the northern side of the Hinnom valley, just across the line from the territory of Judah, which placed it in Benjaminite territory (Josh. 15:1, 8)!

Politically it was the perfect move. If David could rally the support of Saul's relatives in Benjamin, he had the greatest likelihood of winning over Ephraim, Benjamin's closest relatives to the north. Once this the strongest tribe of the nation had solidified in its support, David could expect the whole of the nation to stand behind him in his conflicts with foreign nations that were sure to follow.

And so it was. The blessings of unity were achieved. Brethren dwelt together in harmony. The dew of Mount Hermon, far to the north, began to fall on Mount Zion in the region of the south (Ps. 133:3). God's kingdom of peace and prosperity began to take shape under the Lord's appointed ruler.

But it must not be supposed that Jerusalem's location was determined simply because young King David was a shrewd politician. The choice of Jerusalem had far deeper roots. Jerusalem had been the place of the most significant sacrificial act of worship offered in Israel's ancient history, and from the beginning it seems that David had in mind the relocation of the nation's central place of worship as well as the relocation of his own throne. After a three-day journey, possibly from the edge of the desert at Beersheba, Abraham had arrived at Mount Moriah to present his own son as a sacrifice to God. According to the Lord's command, Abraham had offered his son at the designated spot, and his son did not resist being offered.

But God provided for himself a sacrifice. In this mountain, the very mountain where David subsequently chose to locate his throne in Israel, Abraham had offered his only son and received him back again. It was just as though Isaac had died and been raised again to life (Gen. 22:9–14; Heb. 11:17–19). At this same place, David also offered his own sacrifice, a sacrifice to turn aside the wrath of God from the nation (1 Chron. 21:25–26).

All along, David seems to have envisioned the merger of his throne with God's throne. He intended to build a house for his God at the capitol city of his kingdom (2 Sam. 7:1–3). Perhaps it was with this expectation that David built his palace downward from the crest of the hill. The larger area above him he would reserve for the house of God, the resident temple of the Lord where sacrifices would be offered daily for generations to come. Then finally, in the fullness of time, God himself would make the final great sacrifice for human sin by presenting his only Son, the Son that he loved, to end all other sacrifices. This sacrifice also would be offered in this hallowed place.

Solomon eventually built God's house just as David had desired. It was a magnificent structure. But its tenure had to be limited, just as all other types and shadows of the old covenant era. God could not be contained in a temple made with human hands, however glorious that temple might be, as Solomon himself readily acknowledged (1 Kings 8:27). Notwithstanding all its greatness, the earthly Jerusalem could serve only as a shadow of the heavenly reality (cf. Heb. 12:22; Gal. 4:26).

But the magnificence of the site created confusion in the minds of God's people. It was assumed that since this place had become the dwelling of God on earth, the holy city never could fall. Against this superstition, Jeremiah preached his famous "temple sermon," which almost cost him his life (Jer. 7); and in opposition to this erroneous presumption, Stephen declared that the Most High does not live in houses made by human hands, which did cost him his life (Acts 7:48–60). The same error continues today and must be reproved by urging men to put their trust in God's presence manifested through the incarnation, crucifixion, and resurrection of his Son, rather than in superstitious traditions about a sacred place or people.

Samaria[5]

At the death of King Solomon, Rehoboam his son traveled into the territory of the north for his coronation as king of all Israel. Ancient Shechem was a natural place for the confirmation of his succession to the throne of his father Solomon. Strong appeals came from the people for a gentler touch from their monarch at that critical point of transition in power. A stiffening by the new king was the wrong policy for the moment, and schism was the result. Jeroboam, from the strong tribe of Ephraim, led the people of the north in the formation of a new empire with its capitol in Shechem. Under Baasha's rule its center was moved to Tirzah (1 Kings 15:33; but cf. 1 Kings 14:17),

---

5. For further treatment of Samaria, see p. 118

and then with the beginnings of the dynasty of Omri it was situated in Samaria (1 Kings 16:24).[6]

These three locations—Shechem, Tirzah, and Samaria—are all close to one another, located in the valleys and nearby plains outlined by the mountains of Gerizim and Ebal. The very fact that the northern kingdom of Israel had three centers of government within a few short years tells a tale in itself. God had not pointed to a place for them as he had done for the kingdom of Judah (cf. Deut. 12:5–7, 11–14, 18, 21, 26). Each new locale represented the violent emergence of a different royal family, in contrast with the stability established by the singular dynasty of David in the south. In addition, the northern kingdom never effectively merged the civil centers of the nation with its religious center, as King David had done with the bringing of the ark of God's covenant to Jerusalem. To please the people and to divert their regular pilgrimages to Jerusalem, Jeroboam set up his own centers for worship at Dan to the north and at Bethel to the south. With a different religious calendar and a non-Levitical priesthood of his own choosing, he hoped to divert the loyalty of the people away from David's descendants as they continued to reign in Jerusalem (1 Kings 12:26–33).

Jeroboam and his successors in the north led the people into a pattern of false worship and corrupt morals. Eventually they introduced such corruption that exile from the Lord's land was inevitable.

Samaria played a prominent role in this whole process of degradation. The city was built and embellished by Omri, Ahab, Ahaziah, and Joram, whose combined reigns repre-

---

6. Significant evidence of Israelite occupation has been uncovered by extensive excavations at Samaria. Archaeologists have identified six Israelite periods beginning with Omri and ending with the city's destruction at the hands of the Assyrians in 722 B.C. Israelite construction and masonry have proved to be of outstanding quality. The royal quarter of the acroplis included two main fortification systems and a building considered to be part of the palace of the kings of Israel. The so-called "ostraca house" contained numerous inscribed potsherds.

sented the second-longest dynasty of the northern kingdom. For approximately fifty years, the expansive and corrupting policies of the Omriad dynasty controlled the mindset of the northern kingdom. Ahab in particular embodied the syncretistic policies that merged the depraved practices of Tyrian Baal-worship with the pure worship of the holy God of Israel. It was Jezebel, Ahab's queen from the coastal city of Tyre, who set the worship of the gods of Baal alongside efforts to honor the covenant LORD of Israel.

This capital city of Samaria was located on a large, rounded hill in the center of a broad valley leading westward toward the Mediterranean. It became a major point of governance for this territory centuries later in the days of the Romans, even as it had served the Israelites in the days of the divided monarchy. On this site, Ahab built his famous ivory palace (1 Kings 22:39). At the gates of this city, Ahab of Israel and Jehoshaphat of Judah sat on their thrones in all their splendor while Micaiah the prophet predicted that King Ahab would die in his battle against the Arameans at Ramoth-Gilead (1 Kings 22:10, 28). Though he disguised himself for the battle, an arrow shot at random found its mark in the joints of Ahab's armor as he raced across the battlefield in his chariot. In partial fulfillment of a prophecy spoken by Elijah, the dogs licked the blood of Ahab from his chariot at his return to Samaria (1 Kings 21:17–19; 22:38).

Eventually Samaria came under siege for a period of three years when the land was invaded by Shalmaneser, king of Assyria. In 722 B.C., the city fell to Sennacherib of Assyria and was burned to the ground, with all its principal citizens either killed or carried into captivity.

Jezreel

Jezreel was noteworthy as the winter palace of Ahab and Jezebel. Located strategically on the edge of the plain of Esdraelon, Jezreel guarded the valley that led downward to

Beth Shan. Ahab showed his smallness when he coveted the vineyard of Naboth that lay adjacent to his royal palace in Jezreel. The king pouted when his neighbor honored the law of Moses by refusing to sell his land, and asked no questions when Jezebel declared that she had a way of satisfying his inordinate desire (Lev. 25:23; 1 Kings 21:7). This she did by having their neighbor Naboth stoned on the basis of false testimony offered by hired witnesses. But neither Ahab nor Jezebel could escape the just ways of the Lord. Right at the place where the blood of innocent Naboth had been spilled, dogs would lick the blood of Ahab and Jezebel (1 Kings 21:19, 23–24).

In view of even a limited repentance on the part of Ahab, he personally was spared the full humiliation involved in the fulfillment of this prophecy (1 Kings 21:27–29). Nevertheless he perished in battle as the prophet of the Lord had predicted, and dogs licked the blood from his chariot in Samaria (1 Kings 22:35–38). But subsequently, at the hands of Jehu, the life-blood of both Jezebel and her son Joram was spilt at Naboth's vineyard (2 Kings 9:25–26, 36–37). This luxurious winter palace of the kings of Israel made noteworthy as the locale where the Lord manifested his just ways in dealing with sinners.

Megiddo

Solomon fortified Megiddo, along with Hazor and Gezer, as one of those points critical to the security of his nation (1 Kings 9:15).[7]

---

7. Solomon's fortification of Megiddo is well attested by archaeology. At the top of the ramp providing an approach to the city was a sharp right-angled turn that led to the gate of the town. The entrance featured a typical Solomonic, six-chambered complex, a style duplicated at Hazor and Gezer and dating to the period of the united monarchy. Just east of the gate was a palace apparently built by Solomon, and a large casement wall by which the king fortified the city. Excavations indicate that Megiddo was a bustling city during Solomonic times. Evidence of formidable destruction of the Solomonic building covers the site, which may be assigned to the invasion of Pharaoh Shishak in c. 925 B.C. This conclusion has been supported by the discovery of a Shishak stele on the mound itself.

As neighbor to Jezreel, Megiddo also guarded one of the passes connecting the broad valleys of Galilee with the coastal plain leading along the Mediterranean toward Egypt. Armies marching from the north through Palestine toward Africa almost invariably would pass under the shadow of Megiddo's fortifications. Even today, modern highways shuttle countless automobiles near the ancient site.

For the remnant of Israel living in Judah, Megiddo became a focal point of great national sorrow. For there the last godly king of Judah perished in 609 B.C. Good King Josiah insisted on intercepting Pharaoh Necho of Egypt as he marched northward. Josiah's purpose may have been to halt the alignment of Egypt's forces with the weakened remnants of an Assyrian army already beaten badly by the Babylonians. The pharaoh of Egypt appears as a strange medium for the word of God addressed to a godly king like Josiah. But in this case his warnings originated with the Lord. They went unheeded by Josiah. This good king perished needlessly, and was lamented bitterly by Jeremiah, who saw Israel's last human hopes fading with the king's expiration (2 Kings 23:29–30; 2 Chron. 35:20–25).[8]

Jeremiah's lament took on eschatological proportions in the postexilic prophecies of Zechariah as he anticipated a future day in which the nation would weep at the fatal wounding of one greater than Josiah (Zech. 12:10–12). Ultimately the locale of Megiddo was identified symbolically as the site of the last great struggle between the forces of God and Satan

---

8. Remains at the site of Megiddo that date to the divided kingdom are numerous. On the southern section of the mound, a large grain silo dating to the period of Omri-Ahab has been uncovered. As evidenced by the remains, a series of tripartite, pillared buildings probably served as storehouses or stables during the time of Ahab. In addition, excavation has uncovered an elaborate tunnel seventy meters in length that ended at a spring outside the city. Megiddo continued to be a prominent city throughout the period of the divided monarchy, maintaining the role it had played during Solomonic times.

(Rev. 16:16). Armageddon draws on the past strategic significance of this city to anticipate the day when God's Messiah shall triumph gloriously over all God's enemies. It should not be expected that at this particular pass in Palestine military forces representing God and Satan will exchange blows with rockets armed with nuclear warheads. As broad as the valleys stretching before Megiddo may appear, they could not house the kind of struggle described in Scripture. But the many confrontations staged at this site are fitting figures for the coming Day of the Lord, when the reigning Christ will destroy all his enemies with the breath of his mouth. If Josiah fell as a clear demonstration of the imperfections of even the best of ancient Israel's anointed monarchs, Jesus will stand victoriously in triumph over all his and our enemies.

Lachish

Once the international warlords of Assyria and Babylon had displayed their supremacy at the pass of Jezreel or Megiddo, they faced little interference from Israel as they marched along the Sharon plain into the territory of Philistia. Only when they turned upward and eastward toward the hill country of Judea were they confronted with heavily fortified resistance. Along each of the valleys leading toward Jerusalem was a strengthened position set to intercept any ambitious intruders.

The city of Lachish lay dead center in the path formed by one of the major valleys leading to the Judean interior. Rehoboam, son of Solomon, reinforced the city as one of his major defense points (2 Chron. 11:5–12). A wall almost twenty feet wide surrounded the summit of the mound on which the city stood. Fifty feet down the slope a second wall thirteen feet in width encased the city. Because of its strategic significance, these elaborate defenses of Lachish appear to have been maintained throughout the succession of Judean monarchs. For once Lachish was taken, the interior heartland where Jerusalem was located lay exposed to direct assault.

Just twenty years after the northern capitol of Samaria had fallen in 722 B.C., Sennacherib, king of Assyria, returned to claim Judah as well. In 701 B.C. he was at the point of launching a major assault against Jerusalem. Lachish was one of the last cities to be besieged. If the Assyrian forces could destroy its defenses, no support could come to interfere with an assault on Judah's capitol (2 Kings 18:13–17; 2 Chron. 32:1–9; Isa. 36:1ff.).

The taking of Lachish gave Sennacherib such a sense of accomplishment that he ordered a gigantic carving in stone to commemorate his victory. This large relief, now located in the British museum in London, depicts with vivid accuracy the shape of the mound on which Lachish was built, the location of the city gate, and the panicked state of the defeated inhabitants— all from the perspective of the nearby hillock on which Sennacherib had situated himself to observe the progress of the siege. Not so accurate is Sennacherib's description of his "defeat" of Jerusalem on this same occasion. He boasts that he "shut up Hezekiah in Jerusalem like a bird in a cage" (Pritchard 1950, 287–88). The statement is accurate as far as it goes. But the inference that Sennacherib actually took Jerusalem is altogether misleading. Instead, his army was mysteriously decimated while camping about the city (2 Kings 19:20–37; Isa. 37:21–37). The mighty king of Assyria had to return to his own land to deal with domestic unrest, only to be murdered by his own sons in the house of his gods (Isa. 37:38).[9]

---

9 Archaeological finds at the site of Lachish shed significant light on events of the eighth century B.C. In this period one of the kings of Judah renovated Lachish and turned it into a well-defended fortress. A double defense wall surrounded the city. The only entrance to the town was through a double gate approached by a ramp that paralleled the outer walls. Inside the wall, a huge palace-fort stood on a raised platform. The Sennacherib Relief from Ninevah portrays an Assyrian assault of the city in great detail. Sennacherib built a seige ramp on the southwestern corner of the city and destroyed its defenses by the use of archers, infantry, and battering rams. A countersiege ramp on the inside of the southwestern corner uncovered by archaeologists indicates the effort made by Judeans to bolster their defense against the Assyrian onslaught. This strenuous attempt at resistance was to no avail.

By the intervening grace of God, Jerusalem had withstood this deadly assault by the Assyrians. But unfaithfulness to the covenant made it impossible for the city to stand forever. Though the one place on the earth chosen by the Lord, Jerusalem was not immune to the Lord's disciplines. Just a little over one hundred years later, King Nebuchadnezzar of Babylon marched along the same trail as the Assyrians before him. Having taken all the smaller cities that offered resistance, Nebuchadnezzar set up his siege instruments against Lachish before launching an assault against Jerusalem. Twenty-one fragments of inscribed pottery, known as the "Lachish letters," vivify the last days of the city before its fall. One letter ends with the statement, "and let [my lord] know that we are watching for the signals of Lachish, according to all the indications which my lord has given, for we cannot see Azekah" (Lachish Letter #4; cf. Pritchard, 1950, 322). This statement accords precisely with the reference in Jeremiah to Lachish and Azekah as the last cities to fall before the Babylonian forces turned their attentions to Jerusalem (Jer. 34:7). The pitiful note from the watchman indicates that he was looking throughout the night in the direction of Lachish for some sign that they had been able to resist the assault of the conqueror from Babylon. But that last ray of hope was now being extinguished, and little possibility of restraining ruthless Nebuchadnezzar remained. Once Lachish fell, Jerusalem's collapse was almost sure to follow.

In 586 B.C., the chosen city of the Lord fell before its enemies. With neighboring nations standing by to mock, the blood of God's servants ran through the streets of the holy city. The walls of the city, the palace, and the temple itself were totally destroyed. So the Lord openly displayed the folly of those who might presume to hide behind Jerusalem's favored status. Past favors of God's grace can never guarantee the sinner that he will be exempted from the righteous judgments of the Lord.

After the prophetically prescribed seventy years of captivity had passed, the people of the Lord returned to their land (2 Chron. 36:21; Jer. 29:10; Dan. 9:2). The language of the contemporary prophets described the events in ecstatic terms. Jerusalem would be inhabited as a city without walls, though a wall of fire would surround it (Zech. 2:4–5). The restored temple would have a greater glory than Solomon's temple with all its splendor (Hag. 2:9). Return to the land meant restoration of paradise and resurrection from the dead (Ezek. 37:11–14).

But things did not appear to be happening quite that way. Fewer than fifty thousand captives returned. The small scope of the restored temple led those who could remember the past glory of the first temple to weep (Ezra 3:12).

Yet there was a germ of truth in the poetic picture of the prophets. For a different kind of glory would come to the restored temple. The Messiah himself would come, more lastingly embodying in himself the glory of God. His own body would be a temple greater in glory than any structure built by human hands (John 2:19–22). The time was coming for the land of the Bible to entertain its most glorious guest.

CHAPTER NINE

THE LAND OF THE BIBLE
IN THE AGE OF
THE NEW COVENANT
(Approximately 5 B.C.–A.D. 100)

This land was made for Jesus Christ. All its diversity was designed to serve him. Its character as a land bridge for three continents was crafted at Creation for his strategic role in the history of humanity. Even today all nations flow constantly to this place, for it is uniquely his land, the focal point of the world.

In considering the land of the Bible in the age of the new covenant, it is necessary first to set the stage for the entry of the principal player, who is Jesus Christ, God incarnate.

For at this critical moment, the stage of human history was not by any means vacant. Though there is only one unique Son of God, he has many rivals. Three of them were prominent at the time of Christ's coming into the world: the Caesars, the Herods, and the leadership of the Jewish nation.

The Caesars of the new covenant era were not backward in accepting the proposal of their people that they regard themselves as gods. How could their total control over all the nations of the world be explained otherwise? They had conquered the known world of their day, including the land of Palestine. They put their indelible mark on the land with roads, aqueducts, amphitheaters, temples, palaces, statuary, and cities. In the days of Jesus and his apostles, Roman law governed the life of the nation. These laws had significant effects on the birth, life, death, and ministry of Christ and his apostles.

Of course, Scripture makes it plain that the God of heaven and earth rules and overrules in all the affairs of men despite their vigorous self-assertions. Never under any circumstances does he relinquish his control of all the affairs of his creation. He does as he will among the armies of men and the inhabitants of earth, and "no one can hold back his hand or say to him: 'What have you done?'" (Dan. 4:35). During the life of Christ on earth, these mighty monarchs schemed and raged against the Lord and against his Anointed One. But in the end, they only served the preset purposes of the eternal, gracious, good, and sovereign God.

The Herods who ruled in the times of the new covenant also put their mark on the land of the Bible. Herod the Great (37–4 B.C.) was consumed with a passion for construction. Partly to please the Jews, partly to satisfy his own penchant for pleasure, and partly out of a paranoid fear that men were seeking his life, Herod built and built and built. He erected magnificent structures among the mountains of the north and into the desert of the south, from the shores of the Mediterranean to the edge of the Dead

Sea. Everywhere that Jesus and his disciples went, the marks left by King Herod were evident.

The third rival to Jesus' claim on the land of Palestine was epitomized in the leadership of the Jews. Their nationalistic aspirations inevitably came into conflict with the true purposes of God as manifested in Jesus Christ. Though living under Roman authority, they retained certain powers of self-determination that they had no intent of relinquishing. As one contemporary describes their perspective on the ministry of Jesus in relation to their own powers of national self-determination, "If we let him [Jesus] go on like this, everyone will believe in him, and then the Romans will come and take away both our place and our nation" (John 11:48). This statement in the original text of Scripture emphasizes the possessive pronoun: "It is *our* place and *our* nation that the Romans will take away because of him." Repeatedly this sense of possessiveness manifests itself among the Jewish leadership, driving them eventually to call for Christ's crucifixion.

So the stage is set for the struggle over ownership of the land. To whom does this territory belong? Is it Caesar's, claimed by virtue of Roman power, presence, and productivity? Is it Herod's, functionally his as a consequence of his political astuteness in surviving the pressures of both the Romans and the Jews? Does this land belong irrevocably to the Jewish nation as a consequence of the promises spoken to the fathers, giving them an inherent right of possession in every age? Or could this land called Palestine actually belong to Jesus of Nazareth, the teacher from Galilee who walks as a peasant across its varied acres, owning nothing and yet acting as though he possesses all things?

Now consider some of the major words and works of God's Son as he moves about the land the Lord prepared for him from before the creation of the world. Contrast the claims of his rivals to lordship over the land. Follow him as he moves from one place to another, and see whose land it really is (see Map 9).

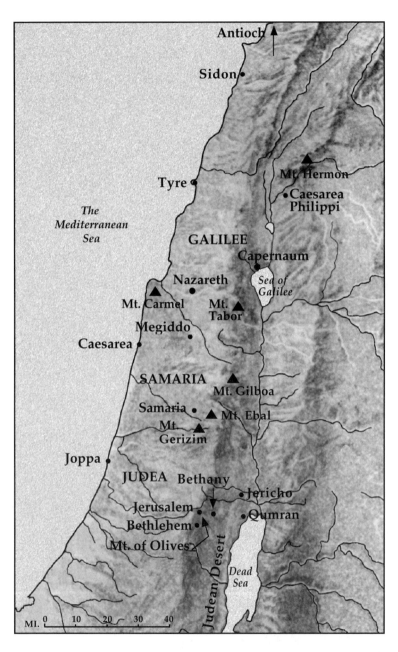

Map 9. The Land of the Bible in the Age of the New Covenant

Nazareth

The announcement that the fulness of time had finally come was delivered first to the Virgin Mary in the town of Nazareth. "Nazareth! Can any good come from there?" was the saying that haunted Jesus throughout his ministry (John 1:46). A visit to the site of the city even today helps explain the statement. Off from every beaten path, up steep winding roads whether the city is approached from north or south, Nazareth was essentially unknown to the people of the old covenant. But it was the place where God's messenger delivered the word to Mary. While still a virgin, she would conceive a child to be known as Immanuel, God with us.

To the relative safety of this out-of-the-way village, Jesus returned as a young child after having fled for his life to Egypt. Hidden in obscurity among the folds of Nazareth until he reached the age of about thirty, Jesus could look across the valley and consider the lives of many of Israel's previous kings. He could view Mount Gilboa where Saul, the first of Israel's anointed kings, had fallen tragically in battle. He could look westward toward Mount Carmel where Elijah had staged his confrontation with Ahab, the worst of Israel's kings. He could also look toward the pass of Megiddo where Josiah, the last of Judah's good kings, had met his early end at the hand of Pharaoh's troops. Not since Josiah's tragic fall six hundred years before the birth of Jesus had a righteous king reigned in Israel.

Jesus was known familiarly as the carpenter's son, and one of the first places where he began to reveal his unique mission to men was in his home town. But when he explained that God's purposes for the salvation of men might embrace the gentile peoples even before the Jewish, his own folk were incensed. Jesus proved his point from the Jewish Scriptures by reference to the salvation that had come to a Canaanite widow and a Syrian general rather than to equally needy people of the Jews (Luke 4:25–27). But these facts made little impression on the people of Jesus' home town. In their minds, the Jewish people existed without rival as the favored ones of the world. If Jesus intended to promote any other perspective, he could forfeit even the right to continued existence.

Bethlehem

Jesus' coming into the world was first announced to his parents in their home town of Nazareth. But Bethlehem had to be his birthplace, for the prophetic word indicated specifically that Israel's messianic ruler would come from the hometown of David (Mic. 5:2). In the Judean wilderness near that town, the king of the Jews had constructed an imposing fortification known as the Herodian. Herod had built a line of fortresses to provide security when he was in retreat from an imagined enemy. The king's vast building projects were designed to protect him from any eventuality. But King Jesus came into this fortified region as a vulnerable infant, seemingly defenseless against the assaults of Herod and his henchmen. Only God himself could have arranged things so that shelter for his Son would be provided under the auspices of the heathen pharaoh of Egypt (Matt. 1:13–15).

In a fallen world, the wailing that accompanied Herod's slaughter of Bethlehem's infants might be regarded as a tragic commonplace. But in this instance, God preserved his Son for a greater sorrow that eventually would provide deliverance for a great multitude from many nations.

The Wilderness of Judea

Two significant events in the early life of Jesus were associated with the wilderness of Judea: his baptism and his temptation. Both of these events confirmed the fact that Jesus was the Son of God.

John the Baptist summoned his entire generation "into the wilderness" in order to prepare the way for the coming of the Lord. If the people were truly repentant of their sins, they should stand ready to renounce the things they possessed and come out into the wilderness to be washed. Prior to John's appearance, an entire community had settled in the barren cliffs along the Dead Sea as a protest against the corruptions of the Jerusalem priesthood. Known today as the Qumran community, these people were waiting in the wilderness for their idea of a coming messiah. According to the Damascus Document, it was expected that Moses would reappear and lead them a second time through the wilderness into possession of the Land of Promise (cf. Jeremias 1967, 4:861).

Jesus came to John the Baptist in the wilderness. There he was baptized as a way of identifying with his people in their need for cleansing from the defilements of sin. As the Son was praying, the Holy Spirit rested on him in bodily form while the voice of the Father declared, "You are My beloved Son; in You I am well pleased" (Luke 3:21–22 NKJV). In this manner, the triune God himself formally confirmed the person and work of the messianic Son. As God's unique Son, he would rule over all powers on behalf of his people (Ps. 2:7–9), while also taking on the awesome task of the "suffering servant" in whom God was well pleased (Isa. 42:1; 53:12). The Spirit would equip the Son with all the resources necessary for fulfilling his task, and the Father would confirm to the world through all the ages that this One was unique as heir of the world. In the wilderness of Judea at Jesus' baptism, this revelation was given regarding the true heir to the land.

Also in the wilderness, Jesus was tested regarding his sonship to God by the Devil. In the Garden, Adam failed the test of the Tempter, choosing self-determination over submissiveness to God. Israel, after its deliverance from Egypt, also succumbed to complaining against the will of God in face of the deprivations of the desert. Though called God's "son," the chosen nation put God to the test ten times over as they wandered in the wilderness. But Jesus succeeded in the wilderness where both Adam and Israel had failed. Although denied bread and water for forty days and nights, he chose to submit to the will of the Father. He would not accept Satan's offer of instant, painless possession of the kingdoms of the world as a way of avoiding the curse of the cross. Though his deprived circumstances were against him, he overcame temptation in the wilderness and so proved that he was uniquely the Son of God.

Capernaum

It was at the arrest of John the Baptist by Herod Antipas that Jesus traveled to Capernaum "by the sea" to begin his ministry (Matt. 4:12–13). At this place in Galilee of the Gentiles, Jesus announced that the "kingdom of heaven" was at hand. Jesus saw in the arrest of John the Baptist a foreshadowing of what the Jews ultimately would do with him. He responded by inaugurating his ministry in a place and a manner that clearly communicated its worldwide dimensions. He would not be restricted to one nation, but would reach out to all the peoples of the world.

Today among the ruins around the ancient synagogue at Capernaum stands a monument marked *Via Maris,* the "way of the sea." For Capernaum lay directly in the path of the traveling Gentiles of the world. Jesus could have picked no better spot to symbolize the worldwide outreach of his Gospel.

Most remarkable is the fact that the gospel of Matthew refers to this city as "his [Jesus'] own town" (Matt. 9:1; 13:54). No other place, not even Jerusalem, receives this designation. He was not born in Capernaum, his parents did not live in Capernaum, he did not grow up in Capernaum. But it became "his" town. This place of constant interchange between Jew and Gentile—this was the place that most properly could be characterized as "his."

The Gospel of Mark begins with a busy day for Jesus at Capernaum (Mark 1:21–34). Jesus teaches in the synagogue and casts out a violent spirit. He then goes with James and John to the house of Peter and Andrew, which was near the synagogue, where he heals Peter's mother-in-law of a fever (Mark 1:31). After sunset, the people of the town bring to Jesus all the sick and demon-possessed. The whole of the city gathers at the door as he heals many. For long hours Jesus heard people as they shared their needs and then offered the help that only he could give. This busy schedule must have been repeated many times over as he came in and out of Capernaum, the center of his activity in Galilee.

Prominent among the structures still remaining at Capernaum is the framework of a large limestone synagogue that some archaeologists have dated to the Byzantine period in the fourth century A.D. Pottery from the first century A.D. has been discovered under an older basalt cobblestone floor beneath the nave of the synagogue. This early floor very likely was a part of the synagogue built by a beneficent Roman centurion in the days of Jesus (cf. Luke 7:1–10). This good man sent Jewish messengers to Jesus not for his own benefit but out of concern for one of his servants who was on the verge of death. His Jewish emissaries explained that this man had built their synagogue, loved their nation, and was worthy of whatever help Jesus could give. The attitude of the man himself confirms their evaluation. He does not regard himself as worthy of a visit by Jesus. But being accustomed to exercising military authority himself, he expresses confidence that just a word spoken by Jesus even at a distance will be sufficient to heal his ailing servant. With amazement, Jesus notes that he has not found such great faith even among the chosen nation of Israel.

So the city of Capernaum, with its mixture of Jews and Gentiles, serves well as a vivid anticipation of the constituency of the coming messianic kingdom. A Roman soldier who has built a synagogue for the Jews now receives the benefits of God's saving rule on earth, and is hailed as having greater faith than any current member of God's ancient elect nation.

Yet with all the privileges heaped on this one city, the Messiah's awful woes condemn its inhabitants (Luke 10:13–15).

It might be thought that Capernaum would be "lifted up to the skies" to rival the heavenly Jerusalem since it was adopted as Jesus' own city. But no! This favored city shall be brought to the depths instead. Special privilege never can be used as a basis for assurance of blessing. Instead, greater privilege brings greater responsibility.

Samaria[1]

Samaria plays a significant role in shaping the life and ministry of Jesus. Because of its unique history and geography, this town forever remains as the perfect example of nearby neighbors who are culturally estranged. When the Babylonians completed their work of devastation and deportation, they repopulated the area north of Jerusalem with a mixture of foreigners (2 Kings 17:24–40). These people eventually intermarried with the scattering of unskilled Jews that remained, and they developed their own syncretistic culture and religion. The writer of Kings notes that "to this day their children and grandchildren continue to do as their fathers did" (2 Kings 17:40). Gerizim became their holy mountain, even to the point of being home to a temple intended to rival Jerusalem as a worship center. For all these reasons the Samaritans were despised and scrupulously avoided by the Jews.[2]

But Jesus rejected any prejudicial perspective, though never hesitating to correct Samaritan errors of belief and practice. He set himself to incorporate Samaritans equally with Jews in his kingdom. Contrary to the custom of the day, he

---

1. For further treatment of Samaria, see p. 99.

2. Herod the Great rebuilt Samaria in the Roman style during the first century B.C. He made it into a lavish showplace for his friend and patron Caesar Augustus, renaming the city "Sebaste," the Greek equivalent of Augustus. Excavations have uncovered a Roman style forum and basilica dating to Herod's day. In addition, Herod erected a large temple to honor the Roman emperor. These structures lay directly on top of palaces of the Israelite kings who had ruled from Samaria many centuries earlier.

initiated conversation with a Samaritan woman at a well outside their principal city. This action on Jesus' part resulted eventually in the conversion of a number of Samaritan men (John 4:7–9; 39–41). Later Jesus healed a Samaritan leper along with nine Jewish sufferers and made a strong point out of the fact that only the Samaritan came back to give thanks (Luke 17:11–19). He told the parable of the "good Samaritan" who helped a wounded stranger even when Jewish "holy men" passed by on the other side (Luke 10:29–37). He came regularly to Samaritan villages to proclaim the Gospel of salvation. Even though he was rejected by them because he had set himself to go to Jerusalem, the ascended Jesus included them equally with Jews in sharing the blessings of his outpoured Spirit (Luke 9:51–56; Acts 1:8; 8:4–17).

Samaria still has a significant role to play in the purposes of God, not so much in the small group of the ancient Samaritan clan that continues to exist today, but in the principle concerning the spread of the Gospel that their acceptance by Jesus embodies. The mission of Christ always includes nearby neighbors who may belong to a different cultural group or speak a different language. The suggestion that the Gospel is intended to work only or even principally among homogeneous peoples must be carefully evaluated in the light of Christ's ministry among Samaritans.

Jericho[3]

Ever since the profession of Peter that Jesus was the Christ of God, at Caesarea Philippi, Jesus had been journeying toward Jerusalem (Luke 9:18–22; cf. Matt. 16:13–21). From this farthest point north of his active ministry, he moved steadily through the land of the Bible toward his final destination. One of his last stops before Jerusalem was at Jericho.

In visiting Jericho today, the traveler may observe two

---

3. For further treatment of Jericho, see p. 80.

sites for the city. A mile south from the older mound is the New Testament Jericho, built as a winter capitol by Herod the Great (37–4 B.C.). Jericho could be very unpleasant in summer seasons, reaching temperatures of 120° F. But in the winter, it provided a perfect retreat from the chilling colds of Jerusalem. True to form as a king aspiring to be a builder greater than Solomon, Herod erected elaborate structures that included a luxurious palace, public buildings, and sunken gardens 350 feet in length. Numerous villas were built by the rich who joined Herod in Jericho when the seasons were right.

In this last journey through Jericho, Jesus encountered two pitifully poor blind beggars. The existence of two sites for Jericho may resolve the apparent tension between the record of one gospel that describes Jesus as going out of and the other as going into the city when he met these blind men (Matt. 20:29; Luke 18:35). The bold one named Bartimaeus would not cease disturbing the peace until Jesus stopped to heal him (Mark 10:46–52).

Jesus was now on his last journey to Jerusalem. As he was greeted wildly by the pilgrims streaming through Jericho on their way to celebrate Passover in Jerusalem, he singled out Zacchaeus, one of the wealthiest men of the city. In the villa of this man of the world, now repentant for his many acts of extortion, Jesus dined the day before making his last ascent to Jerusalem where he would be crucified (Luke 19:1–10).

Even at this late hour in his life, the Lord's principal concern was for others rather than himself. Both poor Bartimaeus and rich Zacchaeus were the benefactors of his limitless love for men in all stations of life.

Jerusalem[4]

It is God himself in his Word who describes this city as "Jerusalem, which I have set in the center of the nations, with countries

---

4. For additional treatments of Jerusalem, see pp. 69, 83, 94.

all around her" (Ezek. 5:5). By God's appointment, the city of Jerusalem is set as the focal point of the whole earth. And now as Jesus approaches the city for the last time, all past ages also come to their point of supreme focus. Only with great reverence and awe should this time and this place be approached.

Few travelers to the land of the Bible today have the hardiness to walk from Jericho to Jerusalem, but Jesus did it. He started from eight hundred feet below sea level and ascended to a height of 2,400 feet above sea level, all in a distance of approximately eighteen miles. No question can be raised about the physical condition of the man Jesus. He was indeed the "perfect specimen."

In addition, very few visitors to this region would find it possible to maintain Jesus' pace during the last week of his life. Residing each evening in Bethany on the far side of the Mount of Olives, he descended and then ascended the steep slopes leading to the temple area every day (Matt. 21:17; Luke 21:37).

But what was the point? Why did he make himself so conspicuous to the Jewish people during these days right before Passover? Earlier, Jesus would not go up to Jerusalem because he knew the leaders of the people were seeking to kill him (John 7:1; 11:8). Why does he now expose himself so openly in their presence?

The answer is obvious, and it is made explicit when Greeks come seeking him in Jerusalem during the last week of his life (John 12:20). Repeatedly he had declared, "My time has not yet come" (John 2:4; 7:6, 8, 30; 8:20). But now he says, "The hour has come for the Son of Man to be glorified" (John 12:23). The time has come for him to be "lifted up" in crucifixion, resurrection, and ascension (John 12:32). As a consequence, men from all nations will be drawn to him. He is the cosmic Christ, and the whole of the universe will be affected by his being lifted up. Not just from among the Jews, but from among all the nations of the world, people through all ages and from all continents will be drawn to him.

This lifting up of the Son of God could occur only in

Jerusalem. No other place, no other city could substitute. To the covenant people of God he must come, and by the covenant people of God he must be rejected. Only then could the purposes and plans of God as revealed through all the ages be realized.

So the last week of his life on earth begins with his "triumphal entry" into Jerusalem. Jesus must be rejected as none other than the king of the Jews. Mounted on a donkey as the appointed transport of royalty, he enters the city surrounded by vast public accolades. Up the ascent of the old city of Jerusalem he goes, just as Solomon had traveled on David's mule on the day of his coronation (1 Kings 1:38). Despite the dissent of most of Israel's leadership, he was greeted as the "coming one" who would bring salvation to God's people. Entering the vast plaza of Herod's temple, Jesus asserted his authority as God's Son and drove out the corrupted moneychangers from his father's house.[5] Once again the point is reinforced: "all nations" are included equally in his kingdom, and his father's house must stand as a symbol that welcomes all who call on the name of the Lord.

Jesus' confrontation with the leadership of the people continues all through the week, until finally he is betrayed. In an upper room somewhere in this city, Jesus inaugurates the last, the final, the climactic, the new covenant with his chosen people. Taking the remnants of the Passover meal, he symbolically

---

5. The physical remains of Jerusalem from the time of Jesus are elaborate and impressive. Through archaeological evidence, Herod the Great of the first century B.C. may be identified as perhaps the greatest builder in the history of the land of the Bible. Herod erected an impressive palace known as the Citadel, which boasted an advanced defense system. In addition, he constructed the four-towered Antonia Fortress, as well as an expansive temple for the Jews to replace the meager, run-down, postexilic structure. Some of the Herodian blocks used in the construction of the temple platform measure thirty-nine feet and weigh up to one hundred tons. The Huldah Gates, discovered on the south side of the temple platform, provided access to the peak of the mount. Jesus and his disciples would have entered the temple area through these gates.

substitutes his body and his blood for the offering of the sacrificial lamb. The long, last night has begun. It will be an ex-
hausting time as he trudges sleeplessly down from the city
across the brook Kidron into the Garden of Gethsemane. At
midnight he agonizes alone, is arrested and maltreated. While
it is still dark, and into the early hours of the morning, he is
dragged back and forth across the city. He undergoes six different trials, three religious and three civil. Pilate, the Roman
authority, publicly declares him innocent no fewer than three
times and then turns him over to be beaten and crucified.

The path that Christ followed in crisscrossing the city on
that night cannot be precisely reconstructed. It may have begun at the northern end of the temple area at Antonia's Fortress, then back and forth across the city from the residence
of Pilate to the court of Herod. In any case, he ends up exhausted the next morning. Yet he must bear his own cross.
Several of the traditional fourteen "stations" of the cross are
legendary in nature, but the others may serve to remind of
the agonies he endured throughout that long night: he is
condemned and beaten, he receives his cross, Simon of Cyrene
takes up the cross, Jesus speaks to the daughters of Jerusalem,
he is stripped of his garments, he is nailed to the cross, he dies
on the cross, he is taken from the cross, he is laid in the tomb.

The places now identified as "Gordon's Calvary" and
"Gordon's Tomb" are far more appealing from an aesthetic
perspective than other proposed locales for the death and
burial of Christ. But it is far more likely that Jesus was crucified and buried at the anciently identified place now serving
as the location of the Church of the Holy Sepulcher.
Constantine and his mother began to build a church on this
site in A.D. 326. Inside the church as it stands today is a massive two-story rock protruding from an ancient quarry that
lay outside the first-century city wall. From earliest times this
mound has been identified with the biblical Calvary. A scale-
model representation of this massive rock and its surrounding quarry may be viewed in the modern city of Jerusalem.

Even against the background of the walled city and its Herodian temple, this huge rock called Calvary stands out as a natural phenomenon with a prominence as great as other structures in the area. It is the focal point of all human history, the crux of divine dealings with human depravity, the place of the cross of Jesus Christ. At this place, the Son of God was offered in substitution for the judgment of death that sinners justly deserve. All roads lead to this one place. Here the sinner either will turn away in unbelief and bear the consequences of his own sin, or will cry out for the mercy of God to view the life and death of the Son of God in place of his imperfections.

Right near this place the cosmic event of the resurrection of the Son of God also occurred, an event as significant as the creation of the world. For as the firstfruits of a new creation, Jesus Christ came out of the tomb with a different kind of body, a body permeated by the Spirit of God. This new body could be recognized, felt, and seen; and yet it could pass through closed doors, appear and disappear at will. While having the characteristics of corporate existence, it also participated in the distinctive nature of spirit. Being the first of its kind, this new form of reality is difficult to comprehend, given the limitations of human understanding and experience. Yet by faith today a person can participate in the power of this new life originating in God's Spirit.

To know this new way of living with God, a person must look to the "Jerusalem above," where the resurrected Christ reigns over heavenly and earthly powers. For the present, earthly Jerusalem known to men continues to be in bondage with all her children (Gal. 4:25). The power flowing from the heavenly Jerusalem and its reigning, resurrected King was displayed openly at Pentecost, fifty days after Jesus' last Passover meal. The disciples had been told to remain at this same earthly Jerusalem until they received the promise of the Father. It was in the temple area—perhaps at the broad, southern steps overlooking the old city of David—that visible, audible manifestations of the gift of the Spirit came on the assembled apostles.

These first twelve recipients of the Spirit of the new era of redemption instantly became the vehicles for transporting the new life that had its source in the heavenly Jerusalem. The new Israel of God was born in a day, and soon the worldwide kingdom of the cosmic Christ began to spread into the vast regions occupied by men of all nations. While the Jerusalem of this earth continues in bondage to the corrupting pride of man's sense of personal accomplishment, the Jerusalem above gives birth to men newly freed.

Caesarea

After describing the city of Jerusalem and its central role in redemptive history, the consideration of any other place might seem anticlimactic. But since Christ's ascension to heaven and his outpouring of the Spirit from his new position at the right hand of the Father, the center of operations in the kingdom of God has shifted from the earthly to the heavenly Jerusalem. From this perspective, any point on earth touched by the subduing Spirit of Christ takes on primary significance. So if God's greater work should occur somewhere other than the earthly Jerusalem, then that place of greater work—wherever it might be—takes on the greater prominence.

A sign over the entrance to the temple area in Jerusalem now forbids all Jews to enter, lest they inadvertently trample the Holy of Holies. It was because of his protest against this misunderstanding of the very nature of God that Stephen was stoned. He contended that God could not be localized, confined to Jerusalem, and that the city had no holiness in itself (Acts 7:48–53). For this supposed heresy he was martyred.

The consequences of this rejection of truth concerning God's basic nature came almost instantly and are still being felt today. The persecution that arose after the martyrdom of Stephen scattered the early Christian believers far beyond the confines of Jerusalem and its environs. Although the apostles remained in Jerusalem, many heralds of the saving Gospel of

God fled the city. All nationalities of the world were the bene-factors, but Israel suffered temporal and eternal loss.

In the thoroughly Roman town of Caesarea, located on the Mediterranean Sea north of the modern Yafo (Joppa), a God-fearing Roman centurion named Cornelius lived with his family (Acts 10:1–2). To this gentile soldier of a crack Italian regiment the Lord appeared in a vision. A man named Peter must come up to him from the neighboring seacoast town of Joppa. Meanwhile the apostle Peter, whose travels had brought him to this area, was being taught by the Lord about the new state of the Gentiles in the kingdom of God through a vision of his own. At the Lord's direct command, Peter complied with the request of the centurion's delegation and traveled to Caesarea. As he proclaimed Jesus' death and resurrection, the Holy Spirit came on these gentile hearers just as he had come on the Jews at Pentecost (Acts 10:44–48). Without becoming a part of the earthly Israel, Cornelius—along with all his family and friends—had received the ultimate blessing of the Spirit. God was breaking through human barriers in order to demonstrate his sovereign reign over all the nations.

Today, extensive remains of the marvelous city that was ancient Caesarea may be seen. A magnificent man-made harbor with artificial breakwaters, a temple, a palace, a theater, a hippodrome, and an elaborate aqueduct system—along with remains of an extensive crusader city—all are there. Herod the Great constructed the city in about 22 B.C. according to the pattern of a Roman city and named it after Augustus Caesar. Pontius Pilate had his residence here, and an inscription has been found at the site bearing his name. Here also the Lord showed the superiority of his Word over the proud pronouncements of the dignitaries of the earth. Herod Agrippa, who had just recently inaugurated a persecution of the Christian church by putting to death James the brother of John and imprisoning Peter to please the Jews, came to Caesarea in an effort to settle a running dispute between himself and the people of Tyre and Sidon (Acts 12:1–4, 19–20). Draped in his regal finery, Herod accepted the flattering accolades of the people fawning over him as he delivered his speech. As a consequence of failing to give glory to God, the king was struck dead on the spot (Acts 12:21–23).

But the Word of the Lord continued to increase and spread (Acts 12:24). Herod's rule came to a tragic termination, but the rule of Christ's new kingdom spread from Caesarea and continues to advance throughout the world even today.

The apostle Paul also had significant encounters with the Roman officials at Caesarea. When a plot against his life was uncovered while he was under Roman custody in Jerusalem, the centurion in charge ordered that a brigade of seventy horsemen and two hundred spearmen escort Paul in safety to Caesarea. To nullify the fanatical commitment of more than forty men who had pledged not to eat until they had killed Paul, the troop was commanded to exit Jerusalem at nine o'clock that night (Acts 23:12–24). While in Caesarea, Paul was summoned before successive governors Felix and Festus as well as before King Agrippa. In each case he was required to give testimony concerning his faith (Acts 24–26). All of these significant hearings were held in the city of Caesarea. Eventually, Paul's only recourse was to appeal to Rome. But before he left Caesarea, he had spoken immortal words, words far more lasting than all the monuments of the Roman and Jewish governors that lie in ruins about the city.

I strive always to keep my conscience clear before God and man. (Acts 24:16)

It is concerning the resurrection of the dead that I am on trial before you today. (Acts 24:21)

If . . . I am guilty of doing anything deserving death, I do not refuse to die. (Acts 25:11a)

I appeal to Caesar. (Acts 25:11c)

> It is because of my hope in what God has promised our fathers that I am on trial today. (Acts 26:6)

> Why should any of you consider it incredible that God raises the dead? (Acts 26:8)

> I was not disobedient to the vision from heaven. (Acts 26:19)

> I stand here and testify to small and great alike. (Acts 26:22b)

> I am saying nothing beyond what the prophets and Moses said would happen—that the Christ would suffer and, as the first to rise from the dead, would proclaim light to his own people and to the Gentiles. (Acts 26:22c–23)

> I pray God that not only you but all who are listening to me today may become what I am, except for these chains. (Acts 26:29)

It is through these words rather than through man-made monuments that the city of Caesarea continues to impact the history of the world even until today. The testimony of a solitary apostle of Jesus Christ has proved to have greater force than all the fame of the Caesars.

Antioch

The last of the cities to be considered lies outside the standard boundaries of the land of the Bible. But the ongoing work of God in the age of the apostles of Jesus makes this distant location as significant as virtually any other place in biblical history. This Antioch was in Syria, more than three hundred miles north of Jerusalem. This location as a new focus of the expanding kingdom of the Messiah is particularly striking considering that Jesus journeyed along the coast of the Mediterranean only as far as Sidon, which is less than halfway to Antioch. Even Solomon's kingdom in its most expanded dimensions did not include the region of Antioch.

Yet this city obviously became a determining factor in the course of Christendom. At the persecution arising from the martyrdom of Stephen, some disciples fled as far as Antioch. These displaced believers took the initiative and began to tell Greeks the Good News about the Lord Jesus. When reports of massive gentile conversions in Antioch got back to Jerusalem, the church sent Barnabas to investigate the matter. His arrival resulted in the conversion of numbers more—so many more that a plea for additional help had to be sent to Saul of Tarsus. Barnabas knew Paul well, for he had vouched for him before the apostles in Jerusalem when the rest of the disciples would not let him join their fellowship out of fear that he was not truly converted (Acts 9:26–27). No doubt Barnabas had heard Paul relate the story of his commission to the Gentiles many times over and had witnessed his skill in debating with the Grecian Jews of Jerusalem (Acts 9:15, 28–29). For a full year, this powerful pair discipled large numbers of people at Antioch. This rapidly growing group of converts made such an impact on the city that the name "Christian" was used in Antioch for the first time to designate the disciples of Jesus (Acts 11:19–26).

Additional evidence reinforces the shift in the center of gravity for God's kingdom on earth. A prophet named Agabus journeyed three hundred miles from Jerusalem to Antioch to predict a worldwide famine (Acts 11:27–30). Why wasn't he content to make his prediction in Jerusalem? Very likely this word from the Lord came in Antioch so that these new, enthusiastic believers could help the poorer Christians suffering in Jerusalem. But is it not noteworthy that help should come *to* Jerusalem rather than *from* Jerusalem?

Then the time comes for the Spirit to mobilize the church into a force for thrusting missionaries into the vast expanses of the gentile world. But this dramatic new phase in the life of Christ's church does not originate in Jerusalem. Instead, it is at the distant outpost of Antioch that the impetus comes. The walls of this church bulge with gifted prophets, teachers, and pastors. As they are worshipping and fasting, the Holy Spirit directs the church to set apart Paul and Barnabas for their appointed work of journeying with the Gospel to the gentile world (Acts 13:1–3). After hard but effective labors throughout Asia Minor, this first missionary team returns not to Jerusalem but to Antioch, gathers the church together, and gives a full report of all that God had done through them, explaining how he had opened the door of faith to the Gentiles (Acts 14:26–28).

It is not that Antioch actually takes the place of Jerusalem. But Antioch stands alongside Jerusalem among many other places as critical centers from which the power of Christ's kingdom radiates. Ephesus, Corinth, Philippi, Rome—all of these earthly, cosmopolitan communities serve as satellite centers for spreading the Good News about God's gracious new covenant kingdom. The "new wine" of the new covenant Gospel and its worldwide domain cannot be contained in the "old wineskins" of the limited, typical kingdom structures of the old covenant community. The old covenant Jerusalem that served well in its day as a shadow and type of the new covenant reality has now been superseded by the reality of the Jerusalem that is above, where the risen Christ continues to reign over heaven and earth. The approach of the worshipper today is to a different Mount Zion, to the heavenly Jerusalem where saints and angels are assembled continually to offer praise to God for their redemption by the Christ (Heb. 12:22).

Yet it must not be concluded that the Jerusalem in the land of the Bible has lost all significance in the purposes and the plans of God. Not only in Antioch but also in more distant places of Christ's church, a clear concern was expressed for the suffering saints in Jerusalem (2 Cor. 8:1–4; Rom. 15:25–26).

A concrete bond of fellowship was maintained perpetually between the saints of God scattered throughout the whole empire of Rome and the persecuted saints in Jerusalem. All through the ages, the universal church of Christ has shown its interest in this city, this land, this people.

But now the final question must be asked: How is the land of the Bible to be viewed today? What should be the attitude of Christians in various parts of the world to this place that has played such a prominent role in the history of God's people throughout all ages? A number of answers have been offered to this crucial question, and each of these different perspectives needs to be considered carefully.

PART THREE

CONTRASTING PERSPECTIVES ON THE LAND

Several different perspectives on the land of the Bible have arisen in the course of history. In many ways, these various views of the land belong distinctively to the age in which they developed. Yet it is also true that basic elements of these different ways of looking at the land have been present in every human era and are no less present today than they were when originally established. Five perspectives on the land of the Bible warrant special attention.

CHAPTER TEN

FIVE PERSPECTIVES ON THE LAND

The Crusader Perspective

The energy spent and the blood spilt because of the Crusader perspective on Palestine is almost immeasurable. Almost a thousand years after the misguided Crusaders made their futile attempt to claim Palestine for Christianity, the land still shows the pockmarks that remain as a result of their presence. Remnants of walls, castles, churches, and cities protrude from the surface of the land wherever the traveler goes. At Caesarea, an impressive moat and fortress remain. With a spectacular view overlooking the Jordan valley, impressive remains of Belvoir Fortress still stand. This significant citadel withstood a four-year siege near the end of the twelfth century before it finally fell to Saladin. The shell of a Crusader castle dramatically occupies the peak of a mountain on the way toward snow-covered Hermon, and the ruins of another mark the halfway point on the way down to Jericho from Jerusalem. At Jerusalem itself, large parts of the city wall date back to the days of the Crusaders.

So what inspired this massive sacrifice of life, limb, fortune, and family? Obviously motivations must have been mixed. But undergirding the whole endeavor was the view that this land was holy and therefore could not remain in the hands of a Muslim community. To protect its sacredness, this holy ground must be wrenched from the infidels without regard for the cost.

Few people today would claim that their view of the land of the Bible agrees with the perspective of the Crusaders. Yet one wonders: is not the commonplace designation of this place as the "Holy Land" tainted with the twisted outlook of the Crusaders? Just what is it that makes this land "holy" in the minds of so many? So long as the "Glory," the *Shekinah,* dwelt in the temple of Jerusalem, the land was made holy by the special presence of God. But the departure of the "Glory" meant that the land's holiness, its sanctification by God's abiding presence, was no more. Just as the burning bush in the wilderness sanctified the ground around it only so long as the glory of God remained, so this land was "holy" only so long as God was uniquely there.

Indeed, many people may affirm that they sense a special closeness to God as they "walk today where Jesus walked." But human feeling cannot be equated so simplistically with divine determinations. In fact, the specific teaching of Jesus was that the time would come when the presence of the holy God would be found neither in Jerusalem nor on the mount of Samaria, but wherever he was worshipped in Spirit and in truth (John 4:21, 23). Material locale simply does not have the capacity to retain divine holiness.

The Crusader perspective on the land of the Bible led well-meaning people astray for centuries. It cost countless families their husbands, their children, their fortunes, and their futures. The same misdirected zeal may not characterize people today who think of Palestine as the "Holy Land." But this view can mislead severely and substitute a false form of worship for the true. Instead of accepting the biblical teaching that any location can be the most holy place on earth if the one true God is worshipped through Jesus Christ at that place, the land of the Bible is romanticized so that people suppose that if they are there God will be known with special power and truth.

The Pilgrim Perspective

All through the ages, people have felt a compulsion to travel to the land of the Bible. Most individuals make the trek because they naturally associate the land with the events recorded in the Bible. But throughout history, the motivation of many has been a sense of gaining merit with God. Even in the twentieth century, professing Christians travel halfway around the world to be "rebaptized" in the Jordan River, assuming that somehow this water has a greater capacity for cleansing from sins than any other. A yet more subtle version of this same view supposes that a pilgrimage to the land of the Bible will remove the soul's haze and give a clear vision of the person of Christ.

But Scripture offers no specific blessing for the sinner as a consequence of his traveling to any particular place. Only faith in the sacrifice of God's Son can bring peace between God and men, and this faith can be exercised equally from any place in the world. It actually brings into question the sufficiency of the sacrifice of Jesus Christ to suggest that some physical relocation of the sinner will contribute to restoring him to fellowship with God.

The Zionist Perspective

The rebirth of the state of Israel in 1948 has rejuvenated the belief on the part of many Jews and Christians that the land of Palestine belongs forever to the Jewish people, and that all this land should be returned to them as its rightful owner. On the basis of the promise given to Abraham that the land belonged to him and his offspring forever, it has been concluded that the whole of the land of the Bible remains irrevocably entrusted to the Israelite people. This view has received strong impetus since the termination of World War II. Having witnessed the Holocaust in which six million Jews perished under Adolf Hitler's "final solution" to the Jewish "problem," the Western nations of the world have sympathized with the concept of a Jewish homeland. Early considerations proposed Uganda, among other places, as a possible location for displaced Jews. But in the end, everything pointed to the land of their ancestors. First in trickles against armed opposition and then by the tens of thousands, Jews from every part of the world flowed into the land of the Bible. The visitor today cannot but be amazed at the determination of these people who have come to the land. On the tops of obscure mountains, in the midst of barren deserts, up high-rise apartments among others who do not understand their speech, Ethiopian Jews, Russian Jews, Moroccan Jews, British, Canadian, and Spanish Jews live together. Despite world criticism and complaint, the Jewish people continue to claim this land as their own.

But in what sense is the land, the whole of the land of the Bible, the property of the Jews by right of divine gift and covenant? This question is answered in different ways today even by the Jews themselves. Some among the Hasidim (the most devout of the Orthodox Jews) insist that, by the covenant with Abraham, God gave the whole of the land to Abraham's descendants in perpetuity. Others would be more modest in their appeal to the promises given to the patriarchs. To them the promise of the Lord insures some right of possession for the Jewish nation today, although their claims would not exclude the possibility of political compromise.

There is of course the difficult, unsolved problem concerning the identification of a "Jew." For as a Jewish commentator on Genesis has noted, the "Jewish" people never have known "purity of blood" (Jacob 1974, 233). Since the time that God established his covenant with Abraham, any Gentile could become a full-fledged Jew by confessing the God of Abraham and, in the case of a male, being circumcised (Gen. 17:12–13). The prevailing definition of a Jew as anyone who has a Jewish mother may have some functional appeal. But since the time of Abraham, a "Jewish" mother might have had not one single drop of Abrahamic blood running through her veins. The place of Rahab the Canaanitess and Ruth the Moabitess in the honored line of Davidic kings makes the point rather dramatically (cf. Josh. 6:25; Ruth 4:13–17; Matt. 1:5).

But if any Gentile can become an heir of the promises to Abraham without having any ancestral connection with the Jewish people, then the criterion for inheriting the land cannot be racial. It is not true to the teaching of the Scriptures to say simply that the racial descendants of Abraham are the rightful heirs to the land of Palestine, for the term "Jew" cannot be confined to categories of race.

The "religious" test also proves inadequate in determining who is a Jew, even from a Jewish perspective. Many Jews in the land of Palestine today are atheistic, agnostic, and even antireligious in their personal sentiments. Yet they are recognized by the state of Israel as being "Jewish." As a consequence, fidelity to the religion of Judaism will not be accepted by the Jews themselves as the proper criterion for determining who is heir to the promises of the land.

This question also is difficult to answer from a Christian perspective. The apostle Paul, recognized in his day as a "Hebrew of Hebrews" (Phil. 3:5), declared, "He is not a Jew who is one outwardly" (Rom. 2:28 NASB). Only the person with a converted heart may legitimately be called a Jew (Rom. 2:29). The point could hardly be made more emphatically. If inheritance of the land is associated with being Jewish, and true Jewishness requires the renewal of the heart, then anyone who has no change of heart automatically is excluded from being heir to the promises of God. Contrariwise, every converted Gentile has become a fellow citizen, a fellow participant, a fellow heir of the promises of God alongside Jewish believers in Jesus (Eph. 2:19; 3:6). "For it is we who are the circumcision, we who worship by the Spirit of God, who glory in Christ Jesus, and who put no confidence in the flesh" (Phil. 3:3). Whatever the promises of God to Israel might have been, they now belong to all who have the renewed heart, whether they are Jew or Gentile in background.

Zionism, whether of a Jewish or Christian variety, has tended to blur these considerations about heirs of the promise to Abraham concerning the land. It has been assumed that this promise was directed by God to a race of people called the Jews, while failing to recognize that ancestry never in itself identified the heirs of the promises to Abraham. All through the ages, "Gentiles" could become "Jews" by professing faith in the God of Israel. At the same time, "Jews" could be excluded from inheritance in the promises of God and expelled from the land itself if their professed faith in the God of their fathers proved to be false. Already two mass expulsions from the land have proved that point.

The Millennial Perspective

Companion to Jewish Zionism is the Christian millennial perspective on the future prospects for the land of the Bible. One of the classic forms of this view sees a day coming when, in faithfulness to his promises to Israel, God will restore the Jews to Palestine and establish an earthly Jewish kingdom under the domain of the Messiah. It is proposed that this universal kingdom with its center in Jerusalem will be characterized by an enforced peace. In fulfillment of the prophecy of Psalm 2, the Prince of Peace will rule the nations with a rod of iron, quickly subduing all efforts to subvert his righteous reign. On the basis of Revelation 20, it is understood that this great kingdom will last for one thousand years, and so it is called the "millennial" kingdom. While much variety of viewpoint relates to the sequence of events surrounding this messianic earthly kingdom, the basic premise is the same. Messiah will come, and for one thousand years he will enforce a reign of peace in a restored Jewish kingdom with its center at Jerusalem in the land of Israel.

Significant support for this position has been found in the language of the old covenant Scriptures, which speak constantly of the restoration of Israel to their land after the exile. This language is very explicit in describing the rebuilding of the walls, the planting of vineyards, the reunion of the northern and southern kingdoms, and the setting of David on his throne in Jerusalem. Support also may be cited in the definiteness of the description found in Revelation 20 and its indication that Christ will subdue Satan for a period of one thousand years, after which he will be released for a short time. Because of the apparent definiteness of these scriptural affirmations, it may be assumed that this viewpoint will continue to be favored by a large number of evangelical scholars devoted to the inerrancy and infallibility of the Word of God.

Yet some problems basic to this viewpoint must be noted. First among them is the supposition that God continues to view the Jewish believers of the new covenant differently from gentile believers. For one of the central messages of the new covenant Scriptures is the breaking down of the "middle wall of partition" that previously had distinguished Jew from Gentile (Eph. 2:11–14). The origin of this expectation regarding an ending of the distinction between Jewish and gentile believers is rooted deeply in the old covenant itself. After all, before his calling, Abraham was but one more "Gentile," a worshipper of idols on the other side of the river (Josh. 24:2–3). His basic constitution was no different from that of any other "Gentile" who today is called out of darkness into the glorious light of the sons of God. Even before any "Jewish" nation existed, God made it explicit that his elect people would include descendants of Abraham and "foreigners" who were

Gentiles (Gen. 17:12–13). Constantly the prophets of Israel harped on the point that equal honor must be given to all members of God's kingdom, whether Jews or Gentiles. Isaiah the prophet even placed Israel as third behind Egypt and Assyria as the people of God (Isa. 19:24–25). In a most dramatic and prophetic insight, Esau's descendants are declared to be among the nations who will have God's name called upon them, indicating that they will become principal possessors of the promises that first were given to beloved Jacob (Amos 9:11–12).

These considerations of both old covenant and new covenant Scriptures make the concept of a future prominence for "Jewish" believers in relation to their "gentile" counterparts difficult to comprehend. Although most millennialists would decry any suggestion of a second-rate citizenship for gentile believers, the idea of a future inheritance for Jewish believers that in some way is not equally shared with their gentile brothers runs counter to centuries of scriptural revelation that points in a contrary direction. Is it actually to be supposed that the "middle wall of partition" still exists in the mind of God, and is to be erected again? Yet, apart from some expectation of a geographical fulfillment of promises made uniquely to the Jews, the whole idea of a future millennial kingdom loses its point.

A further matter of significance has to do with the nature of the prophecies concerning restoration to the land. It must not be forgotten that Israel as a nation actually was "restored to the land" after seventy years of captivity, just as Jeremiah had predicted (Jer. 29:10). The fact that this restoration did not correspond to the projected grandeur predicted by the prophets only points to a fulfillment beyond anything that could be realized in the world as it is presently constituted. Ezekiel's vision of the restoration arises out of a context that anticipates the total transformation of nature by the resurrection of the dead (Ezek. 37:11–14). Earthly, temporal improvements to the present state of the world simply will not meet the expectations created by prophecies old and new. The description of the restored Jerusalem in these prophecies anticipates a "New Jerusalem" coming down from heaven in the figurative perfections that will endure for eternity, not the temporal provisions of a mere one thousand years. The water flowing out of Ezekiel's temple has the power to freshen the Dead Sea and make it teem with fish (Ezek. 47:6–12). Is not this description a picture of the land of the Bible that breaks the bonds of time and space as we know it, and anticipates the new creation in which righteousness and blessing shall endure forever (Rev. 22:1–2)?

The millennial perspective on the land of the Bible honors the Gospel of Christ by calling Christians today to take most seriously their responsibility to preach the Gospel to Jews as well as Gentiles. For "God did not reject his people, whom he foreknew" (Rom. 11:1–2). Always, in every generation, a significant number of Jewish believers will be grafted back into the true Israel of God. Yet this view of the millennium also has the disadvantage of creating an expectation for some distinctive dealing of God with the Jews in which the land will be theirs in a way that it will not belong to gentile believers.

The Renewal Perspective

At the beginning of this study, it was proposed that the idea of "land" first appeared in the purposes of God with man's experience of Paradise. The "land" of blessing at Creation was the cosmos, the whole of the universe. In Paradise, man as originally created enjoyed all the blessings of land graciously given by his Creator.

A renewal perspective looks once more to paradise as the ultimate meaning of "land." To Israel, a land "flowing with milk and honey" was promised, but Canaan hardly met for them these expectations of paradise. Yet throughout the centuries, this land served well as a figure, a type of what God ultimately would do. In the end, he would give back to a redeemed race the original paradise they had lost as a consequence of sin.

So it should not be surprising to find the new covenant Scriptures interpreting God's promise to Abraham in cosmic terms. The Patriarch would be heir of the cosmos (Rom. 4:13). The whole of the created universe would be his. Not only would his seed be as numerous as the stars; he and his seed would inherit the stars. Along with the heavens, he would also possess the whole of a reshaped, re-formed earth where righteousness prevailed.

It appears that Abraham sensed this fact all along. Scripture testifies that he was "looking forward to the city with foundations, whose architect and builder is God" (Heb. 11:10). It was not merely the possession of Canaan that he anticipated. He looked for a world with a foundation built by God himself, a renewed world that would last forever. Only then would the promises of God the Father concerning the land find their appropriate climax. For throughout their wanderings in the land of Canaan, Abraham and the other patriarchs "were longing for a better country—a heavenly one" (Heb. 11:16).

Conclusion

The land of the Bible serves a purpose that will outlast its own existence. For eternity, people will praise God for many things. But high on the list will be significant praise for his handiwork in creating this land bridge of the continents, this place where he could carry out the work of redemption for sinners from all the nations of the world. As a grand stage set for carrying out the critical events of the drama of redemption, this land served God and man well.

Even today it can offer a great service to the kingdom of Christ. If rightly viewed, it can reinforce, illumine, and dramatize the eternal truths of the Scriptures. It can inspire a deeper love of God's Word and increase a saving understanding of his eternal plan of redemption.

Select Bibliography

Aharoni, Yohanan. *The Land of the Bible: A Historical Geography.* Translated by A. F. Rainey. Philadelphia: Westminster, 1967.

Baly, Denis. *The Geography of the Bible: A Study in Historical Geography.* New York: Harper & Brothers Publishers, 1957.

Bimson, John J. *Redating the Exodus and Conquest.* Sheffield: University of Sheffield, 1978.

Brueggemann, Walter, *The Land.* Philadelphia: Fortress Press, 1977.

Garstang, John. *The Story of Jericho.* London: Hodder & Stoughton, 1948.

Jacob, B. *The First Book of the Bible: Genesis.* New York: Ktav Publishing, 1974.

Jeremias, Joachim. "Moses." In *Theological Dictionary of the New Testament,* edited by Gerhard Kittel. Translated by Geoffrey W. Bromiley, 4:848–74. Grand Rapids: Eerdmans, 1967.

Kenyon, Kathleen. *Digging Up Jericho.* New York: Praeger, 1957.

Pfeiffer, Charles F., ed. *The Biblical World: A Dictionary of Biblical Archaeology.* Grand Rapids: Baker, 1966.

Pritchard, J. B. *Ancient Near Eastern Texts Relating to the Old Testament.* Princeton, N.J.: Princeton University Press, 1950.

Smith, George Adam. *The Historical Geography of the Holy Land.* 1894. Reprint. Gloucester, Mass.: Peter Smith, 1972.

Index of Maps

Index of Places

Index of Scripture